"'No longer are we seeking lost unsaved people, nor are we laboring in the harvest; instead we are raiding one another's churches,' argues Bill Chadwick. The link between evangelism and church growth has been severed because American Christians find marketing their churches to those who already believe far easier than building the necessary relationships needed to communicate the gospel to those who don't.

"Often the best critiques of movements are offered from within by those who desire genuine renewal and reform. This book fits that mold. Using sound theological reflection and the diagnostic tools of the church growth movement itself, Chadwick offers a powerful critique of so-called transfer growth and argues that the connection between authentic evangelism and numerical growth must be reestablished. *Stealing Sheep* is an important work for all concerned about building healthy local churches in the years to come."

ROBERT J. MAYER,
Gordon-Conwell Seminary, Charlotte, North Carolina

"Jesus did not say, 'Go into all the world and shift the sheep.' A prophetic word has come in *Stealing Sheep!* We must target the Great Commission in order to win this generation to Christ. The only sheep to be stolen must come from the enemy's camp, not our own."

DR. TERRY TEYKL, *Renewal Ministries*

STEALING SHEEP

The Church's Hidden Problems
with Transfer Growth

William
Chadwick

InterVarsity Press
Downers Grove, Illinois

InterVarsity Press
P.O. Box 1400, Downers Grove, IL 60515-1426
World Wide Web: www.ivpress.com
E-mail: mail@ivpress.com

*InterVarsity Press® is the book-publishing division of InterVarsity Christian Fellowship/USA®, a
student movement active on campus at hundreds of universities, colleges and schools of nursing
in the United States of America, and a member movement of the International Fellowship of
Evangelical Students. For information about local and regional activities, write Public Relations
Dept., InterVarsity Christian Fellowship/USA, 6400 Schroeder Rd., P.O. Box 7895, Madison, WI
53707-7895.*

*All Scripture quotations, unless otherwise indicated, are taken from the Holy Bible, New
International Version®. NIV®. Copyright ©1973, 1978, 1984 by International Bible Society.
Used by permission of Zondervan Publishing House. All rights reserved.*

Cover illustration: Diana Ong/SuperStock

ISBN 0-8308-2279-8

Printed in the United States of America ∞

Library of Congress Cataloging-in-Publication Data

Chadwick, William, 1955-
  Stealing sheep : the church's hidden problems with transfer growth / William Chadwick.
    p. cm.
  Includes bibliographical references.
    ISBN 0-8308-2279-8 (pbk. : alk. paper)
    1. Church growth. I. Title.
BV652.25 .C43 2001
254'.5—dc21

                                                                    2001024799

24   23   22   21   20   19   18   17   16   15   14   13   12   11   10   9   8   7   6   5   4   3   2   1

19   18   17   16   15   14   13   12   11   10   09   08   07   06   05   04   03   02   01

CONTENTS

Confronting the Issue 7

PART 1

ONE   STEALING SHEEP 17

TWO   BLEATING SHEEP 33

PART 2

THREE   HAVE YOU ANY WOOL? 61

FOUR   COUNTING SHEEP 77

PART 3

FIVE   FLEECING THE FLOCK 105

SIX   THE GOOD SHEPHERD 135

Epilogue 171

Notes 175

Bibliography 185

Confronting
the Issue

As the postmodern church emerges into a new millennium, a new phase of its pilgrimage is taking place. Leaving the adolescent years of burgeoning church growth, the church appears to be giving new value to a Spirit-directed sense of maturity. Christian writers addressing the development of the church are no longer interested in just numerical growth as the ultimate goal of church growth. Other priorities such as ecclesiastical depth and character are coming to the forefront of the discussion.

Pastor Ted Haggard *(Primary Purpose)* seeks to refocus the evangelistic ministry of the church from domestic programming agendas back to conversion growth. Professor David Wells *(Losing Our Virtue)* warns the church about the need for protecting and recovering its theology and morals, for it has flirted precariously with modernity in an effort to attract a postmodern audience. Steve Macchia, president of Vision New England *(Becoming a Healthy Church),* summarizes the energy of this revitalization hour with his analysis of essential key components that help produce church wholeness and balance in ministry. Even Professor Eddie Gibbs of the church growth epicenter, Fuller Seminary, has written *ChurchNext,* recognizing that the church needs to develop more than skills for rapid expansion if it is to develop into an institution that has substance and meaning.

Each of these is pressing the point that it is time for the church and church growth to come of age. This movement seems to go beyond a rehash of old concerns about church growth methods and principles. Rather these writers, including Wells, a solid church growth critic, have grown to appreciate the value of church growth and now seek to usher the movement into maturity. This must be recognized as a wonderful convergence of the body of Christ working together to prepare the bride for the last days that lie ahead.

Stealing Sheep is yet another facet of this movement. Taking up the topic of transfer growth, this book explores the cost Christendom must bear as church members hop from one church to another.

Some transfer growth occurs as the natural result of relocation. That form of transferring of membership is not the subject of this study. Other transfer growth occurs as people flee some form of ecclesiastical abuse, such as false teaching or unethical practices. These issues will be examined as we start to define the boundaries of what is acceptable or even healthy transfer growth. The book's focus will be directed primarily toward transfer growth driven by motivations that do not reflect healthy kingdom practices and values.

Sheep stealing has been the skeleton in the church's closet that nobody seems to want to confront. Filled with hypocrisies and indiscretions, transfer growth remains frontier territory in the church's quest for ethical maturity and wholeness.

It is important for us to understand that church growth pastors and leaders have grown weary of antichurch-growth arguments. Frankly, most criticisms of church growth methodologies and principles have been raised by those who have not earned the right to be heard.

Hardworking pastors and church planters who sacrificially labor to lead the lost to Christ rarely find value in the criticisms leveled against them from the ivory towers of academia. Rebukes from stagnant mainline churches can be perceived as nothing more than fearful responses to the threat of new ministries raiding the flocks of the well endowed. In short, most church growth critics are viewed with suspicion and lack of respect.

It is my hope that the concerns raised in this book will be heard a bit differently. I myself am a church growth pastor. Studying under the likes of C. Peter Wagner, Lyle Schaller, John Wimber, Rick Warren, Charles Kraft, Eddie Gibbs, Roberta Hestenes and Bill Hybels, I have honed the craft of church growth. In my pastoral career I have successfully implemented the tools of church growth to help churches grow significantly, and I have been involved with the church growth movement since the late 1970s.

My concerns about the negative effects of transfer growth and the message I bring come from the perspective of an insider. These are not lofty ideals created on chalkboards or the pangs of jealousy of the recently scorned. This is a cry for integrity and a research project designed in the best tradition of the church growth movement, focusing on solid facts that I hope will establish my findings and earn thoughtful consideration from my colleagues.

Practical experience has taught me that sometimes we make mistakes in church growth. To our credit we dare to try new and challenging approaches to reaching people with the good news of Jesus Christ because we have a strong sense of mission and compassion for the lost. It is not the taking of risks for the sake of the gospel that concerns me. When something is wrong, when a practice does not truly benefit the kingdom but simply gratifies our own desires, are we equally bold in rectifying that mistake as we are in plunging into another experiment?

Stealing sheep is a case in point. It is a mistake to build your ministry by raiding the pews of your neighbor. To my utter shame, I have alienated fellow pastors and weakened their ministries by luring away their flocks. When the tables turned, I have experienced the pain of watching a parish split and seeing other churches happily grow as a result.

For years I have lived a lie, believing that just because our numbers were increasing we were doing the Lord's work. In reality, enabling discontent through escapism, producing distrust among churches and reshuffling membership certificates can scarcely be considered the work of Christ.

On the altar of numerical success I have sacrificed the heart of the church by compromising integrity, maturity, unity, evangelism and love. Now after many years of ministry I wish to right a wrong. Sheep stealing as a church growth philosophy is a violation of Christian ethics. As a church growth tool it is unacceptable, for the honest result of simply recirculating the saints is no kingdom growth at all. The shifting of saints from one church to another is killing the church.

This book, however, should not be viewed as a polemic focused on the church growth movement. On the contrary, it is my observation that every church and denomination is guilty of engaging in transfer growth practices that exploit other ministries. We must face this practice that has permeated not just the church growth movement but the entire kingdom of God. Church growth's sin is that it turned this popular kind of expansion into an art form, making sheep stealing an accepted church growth principle.

How could such a thing happen? Clearly at the inception of the church growth movement the focus was to evangelize the lost. Unfortunately along the way, as growth principles were laid in place, the greatest numerical growth was generated consistently through transfer growth. Gradually turning toward the light of this success, church programming changed and seeking the saved became most churches' "evangelistic" occupation.

This state of introverted proselytizing gravely concerns me. The great press for the evangelization of the world has been detoured as the church's primary occupation has become seeking the sheep that are wayfarers of a neighboring sheepfold. This redirecting of the church's evangelistic energy may be the single most negative facet of transfer growth.

Understandably, many of my colleagues in ministry will hotly deny that transfer growth has worked so significantly to erode the evangelical mission of the church. But the erosion can be painfully proven. What are we willing to do about it?

This issue is the Pandora's box of the church growth movement. It touches on such a vast array of related topics that an epic work would be required to cover them all. At best I can only hope that this book will serve two purposes.

First, the church growth movement must rise to the challenge of growing up. I hope this book will be a positive step in that direction, addressing concerns that others in the evangelical community have expressed about our philosophies and techniques.

Having graduated from Gordon-Conwell Theological Seminary on the U.S. East Coast, I have learned to appreciate the need for solid theology, good exegesis and the value of church tradition. My work at Fuller Theological Seminary on the West Coast taught me that the Holy Spirit is still very active in expanding the gospel in the world today and that the last pages of church history have not yet been written. Merging these two worlds has forced me to be a better pastor. The discipline of asking hard questions while engaging in bold plans will only bless and strengthen growth in the church.

Second, we need to stem the tide of church hopping. When we plant churches, let's see that the lost are the ones who are drawn in. As our ministries grow, let's be sure that we are not contributing to the demise of another church. When new members join our congregations there should be baptisms, or else we are facilitating yet another spin on the church merry-go-round.

Part one confronts the issue of transfer growth both as an accepted practice in the church and as a direct affront to Christ's design for the life of his body. In chapter one I tell the reader my story and how I came to challenge transfer growth as a means for church growth. Chapter two explores questions regarding ecclesiology and the practice of church transfers; it further examines biblical models of what church membership entails and what levels of commitment are expected from people who become a part of the body of Christ.

Part two highlights a stunning discovery in the church growth movement and explores the development and use of statistics in the church. Chapter three looks at the roots of the church growth movement and its rise to popularity—and the shocking discovery of its failure to yield real growth. Chapter four examines how numbers blinded the church to the lack of growth, and the detrimental effects of being fixated on them.

Part three surveys the hidden cost of transfer growth and leads us to consider how to limit and control transfer growth. Chapter five delves into the cost by investigating the seven deadly sins of transfer growth. Chapter six concludes the book with some bold suggestions for how the Christian community should address the issue of church transfers.

How the church grows touches on the core values of the Christian faith. Failure to address transfer growth weakens the true measure of our productivity, both in the lives of the people we are called to shepherd and in our actual contribution to the well-being of the body of Christ. Sheep stealing has prospered far too long under the guise of growth. It must be seen for what it is.

This book never would have happened if Dr. Ray Anderson had not pressed the point that my thoughts and experiences with this topic are important to the church universal. To him I am thankful.

Two other men, however, inspired the heart and soul of this book. Dr. C. Peter Wagner opened up for me the wonderful world of church growth. I have sat spellbound in his classes and am eternally grateful for his love and dedication. He is one Aggie I will never forget.

But this book is dedicated to another who recently finished his work in this world. Dr. J. Christy Wilson, my mentor and friend, awoke in me a heart for missions. It is this uncompromising desire to find the lost that truly is the incentive for the writing of this book. Dr. Wilson once said that even though I was not destined to serve the Lord on foreign soils, my heart for missions and reaching the lost would inspire many. May this book be a small response to those encouraging words and an expression of the heart Christy shared with his students.

I owe an immeasurable debt to Carol, my wife and best friend, and to Ben and Danny for letting Dad finish his work. I also thank Merry for all the copying and proofreading and extra hours she carved out of my schedule so that I could complete this task, and to the prayer warriors who invited God's influence to be felt in these pages.

Finally, I thank the many professors at Gordon-Conwell and Fuller seminaries who equipped me to press on past the ground that they have laid. They are people of integrity who not only taught their students but also lifted them up in prayer. I pray that this book will bless the church and honor their spiritual and academic investment in my life. Now let us begin.

PART 1

1

Stealing Sheep

The LORD sent Nathan to David. When he came to him, he said,
"There were two men in a certain town, one rich and the other
poor. The rich man had a very large number of sheep and cattle,
but the poor man had nothing except one little ewe lamb
he had bought. He raised it, and it grew up with him
and his children. It shared his food, drank from his cup
and even slept in his arms. It was like a daughter to him.
*   "Now a traveler came to the rich man, but the rich man*
refrained from taking one of his own sheep or cattle
to prepare a meal for the traveler. . . . Instead, he took the ewe
lamb that belonged to the poor man and prepared it
for the one who had come to him."
*   David burned with anger against the man and said to*
Nathan, "As surely as the LORD lives,
the man who did this deserves to die!" . . .
*   Then Nathan said to David, "You are the man!"*
2 SAMUEL 12:1-7

The first time I ever stole anything, I was caught. Like yesterday I can remember the wrath of my mother as my childhood playmate ratted on me. I swallowed the pink Bazooka bubblegum in a vain attempt to avoid the consequences of my actions, but true to form, my mom saw through my thin veneer of innocence. That day I trudged along roadsides in rural Vermont in search of a bottle whose deposit would pay for my crime. Mom's point was clear: stealing, no matter how insignificant, is wrong, and you can never justify it.

Sure you can! Justification is the mother of sin. It is the bridge where temptation and opportunity inspire reasoning that bends biblical boundaries, conforming them to our own wants and desires. In this land of half-truths God's intentions are distorted with semantics. The graves of Adam and Eve can be found here.

For church leaders, numerical growth is a powerfully intoxicating justification. It impairs sound judgment and makes you vulnerable to just about anything that will help you achieve your success. Years after my bubblegum misdeed, I learned that stealing for the sake of church growth is often culturally condoned, an accepted practice in many churches.

The next time I stole I was an ordained Christian minister. My booty was no longer penny sweets. Now I was after something far more substantial that I had seen my Christian colleagues pursue. "Sheep"—parishioners in the pew, churchgoers, members of a congregation, active participants in the body of Christ—were the objects of my attention.

The Nature of Sheep

Some were spiritually fat sheep,[1] so well fed that they loathed the same old meals that had brought them health and prosperity thus far. They were in search of some new and exciting dimension in church life, an unidentified something more. Usually bored, these gross underachievers were not often praised and could be easily enticed to transfer their membership by the promise of a new, fulfilling and invigorating experience.

Others were thin, starving animals—members of a church whose pastor preached the same old message every week and offered no spiritual food to the congregation. Devoid of Bible study opportunities or outreach ministries, these believers hungered for affection and a sense of spiritual well-being. They were easily wooed away from their churches by offers to address the most basic of spiritual needs through simple square meals of discipleship or meaningful worship.

Then there were the black sheep: consummate malcontents who were always testing and challenging pastoral decisions, points of theology or any other topic that could elicit controversy. Perpetually ready to escape from their current shepherd, they lived lives of seeking, church hopping and wanderlust.

Last, there were the dumb sheep, the easily influenced that simply followed the flock. Many appeared mesmerized by the opinions and actions of others. Never really having an opinion of their own, they sought security in keeping in line with the latest trends of the majority. They were in the outer rings of the concentric circle; far from engaging with any issues within a church, they would abandon a body simply because others were doing so.

These may seem like grossly exaggerated and even offensive profiles of members of the body of Christ. However, I believe every pastor and Christian leader who reads this material will affirm that he or she has seen each of these kinds of sheep in the course of ministry.

Changing Values

Our culture's influence on the church has generally been underestimated, and such is the case in regard to church loyalty. Materialistic consumption patterns have eroded longstanding practices of church fidelity. No longer are people loyal to the church of their historic roots; the consumer mentality has changed the nature of church commitment. Church has changed from a place where one serves to a place where one seeks services. In the selection of a church home, denominational affiliations are secondary to the question "Does this church meet our needs?"

Unfortunately, needs can be confused with wants, and wants can be brutally subjective. The quest to find a church that addresses one's wants can lead to a perennial cycle of church shopping. Ultimately one shops for the sake of shopping, paying less heed to the functionality of the current church than to the excitement of acquiring a new one.

Richard Peace has pointed out that our culture engages in consumption not to meet any sustaining need but merely for the sake of consumption.[2] "No longer is need the motivation for eating, buying clothing or changing houses, cars or jobs—want, pure hedonistic pleasure, now drives people's passions."[3]

Cornel West blames the culture, at least in the United States, for this new set of values:

> The decade [of the 1980s] brought us the shortsighted choices of highly compensated corporate executives to consume, acquire and merge rather than invest, research and innovate. . . . The unintended cultural consequence of this economic legacy was a spiritual impoverishment in which the dominant conception of the good life consists of gaining access to power, pleasure and property, sometimes by any means.[4]

Certainly the church has felt a significant impact from this new mindset. People have ceased to invest in the long-term, stable relationships that were the backbone of successful church bodies in the past. Today we have moving church bodies filled with church shoppers and ecclesiastical consumers, joining churches for personal gain and leaving them for the same reason.

The McChurch has replaced the traditional home church and its relational values. Fast-food Christians pull up to ecclesiastical drive-through windows, order their McGroups, consume the experience and then drive off, discarding relationships like burger wrappers on the highway of life. Savvy church growth pastors quickly learned that significant growth can occur if a church learns how to market its burgers to capture the appetite of this roving crowd. In some instances merely producing an interesting alternative to the status quo can lead to significant church disaffections.

Raising the Bar
Such was the case in my first ministry. By employing exciting, dynamic church growth concepts in a hitherto sleepy New Hampshire church, we created an environment that evoked the curiosity

of many churchgoing people in our town. Eventually they came to check us out. The difference between our contemporary style and the traditional services offered elsewhere in our town were significant.

Soon some of the younger families who visited our church began shocking their pastors and family members by transferring their memberships out of churches where their great-grandparents had been charter members. They wanted our "hotter" experience. We saw all of these transfers as exciting church growth developments, as our church prospered from the attention.

I did not have to do the dirty deed of aggressively stealing people out of other Christian churches. A significant part of sheep stealing is passive. If you build it, they will come: this saying pertains to more than just baseball fields. Consumers love to check out new models.

Not even when sheep were actively pursued did I have to be involved. My congregation eagerly did it for me! Our church preached growth, and we needed people and resources to make that happen. So our parishioners were eager to invite people to come and try out our Sunday worship service.

Unfortunately, our congregation's concept of filling the church was to invite their friends and family to attend. Thus those they brought in were almost exclusively already churched people. This is a tragic and all too common church growth experience. My sin was one of omission: I failed to respond as my parishioners proselytized the pews of sister churches.

Web of Influence

In hindsight I have come to understand that our members' instinct to solicit already churched people reflects a common evangelical practice. It has roots in an evangelism principle developed by Ralph Winter: "your web of influence." This principle states that people solicit other people predicated on their already existing relationships. Relatives and friends are warm contacts and are easy to invite to a church service; strangers are cold contacts and we are much more reluctant to solicit them.

This web of influence progression originally was applied by Winter as an evangelism model. Christ's witnessing instructions in Acts 1:8 suggest progressive stages of contact: E-0 (for evangelizing of family members), "you will be my witness in Jerusalem"; E-1 (friends), "in all of Judea"; E-2 (same ethnic group), "Samaria"; and E-3 (crosscultural), "and to the ends of the earth."[5] Though this is an *evangelism* model, the same principles are readily adaptable to sheep stealing.

In the sheep-stealing model our web of influence becomes a target group not for evangelistic outreach but for transfer growth. TG-0 represents our inviting our family to transfer to the church we are attending. TG-1 represents inviting our next tier of relationships, our friends, to our new church home. TG-2 would be inviting Christians we casually meet at concerts, church league softball games or other events. Finally, TG-3 is aggressively raiding churches of other denominations or traditions, in an attempt to convert their members to our style of worship or doctrinal beliefs.[6]

The motivations for this shift of evangelistic energies from non-Christian people to the churched has much to do with the ease and fast results of attracting the converted to a new church home. Building a church on true conversion experience takes time, energy and resources; even when it is successful, developing a disciple who contributes to the ministry may take many more years. Transfer growth is easy, often produces positive results and generates immediate assets.

A Blind Eye

In New Hampshire, from a pastoral perspective, the trend of churched people coming to our church was easy to overlook for a variety of reasons. First was the simple sin of omission: I did not want to question or interrupt the surprising growth we were experiencing, so I simply ignored the need for honest assessment of the results of our church growth efforts. I knew our conversion growth did not equal our attendance increases, but I never questioned where the other people were coming from.[7]

I never deliberately set out to grow a church mostly from transfer growth (although some ministries actually do). The tattered and disenchanted newcomers, turned on by our worship experience, elicited in me the same emotions that I used to have for a stray dog or cat that showed up at our farmhouse in Vermont. First you feed them, then you begin liking them, and soon you name them and refer to them as your own. Sheep stealing appealed greatly to my need to provide for, feed and please people.

Second, and far more sinister, my competitive nature and ego were fueled by the growth of our church. My self-esteem was wrapped up in seeing someone select my preaching over someone else's or preferring our worship service to those of other churches in our community.

Our growth was my growth, and I deeply associated my value with the success of this ministry. Growth gave meaning to the countless hours of hard work the ministry demanded. It put our ministry on the community map and met a host of needs in the church and, I thought, in the work of the kingdom.

Third, already churched believers were instant assets to a very stressed ministry. In the growth mode resources are often taxed, and mature Christians brought their talents, tithes and time. They represented an infusion of new human resources, filled with fresh perspectives and energy to support the laborers who were already in the battle.

One could hardly blame us for desiring their help and fellowship. With their support our combined efforts were making a positive impact for Christ in our rural community. Without the support of these believers our growth would have been significantly hampered and many of the programs we ultimately launched never would have happened.

Fourth, there is a common error to which human beings are susceptible: believing truth is revealed through democratic process and majority vote. In our church this occurred when the large influx of Christians began to create the impression that their transferring of membership was an OK thing to do. The simple numbers seemed to impart God's endorsement. Surely if anything were wrong with it, one of these mature believers would blow the whistle. Instead they all justified the sin and joined in supporting one another's decision to transfer to our church. This mass movement had the effect of soundly sealing all doubts about the rightness of their transferring to our church, by creating a false unity of the Spirit in the decision.

This fueled the fifth mistake: because of our growth and popularity among transferring believers, the illusion was created that God's favor was exclusively upon us. This definitely hurt other churches by implying that the Spirit of God was moving in our church and not in theirs.

We were the most popular church in town, and we enjoyed the success, believing that we were providing good things that people could not acquire from their former churches. It was easy, incredibly easy, to believe that the Shekinah glory had found a new home, so who could deny the masses the chance to come and experience it?

Soon we became the "fastest growing church" in our denomination, which would have been a stellar achievement if our growth could have been built on conversions, but it was not. The fame and accolades of my peers fueled an addiction inside me and in the heart of our church.

Numerical growth became our unofficial mission goal. It was the new standard, the measuring device by which we gauged the success of everything we did; it was the be-all and end-all. Christ's commission to save the lost[8] was quickly becoming just a veneer for our true preoccupation with just becoming bigger.

Freedom of Choice
Certainly I never questioned the consequences or the ethics of

having people change churches. Moving from church to church is a Christian tradition predicated on freedom of choice and so widely practiced that "letters of transfer" are standard church administrative fare.

The migration of people from one church to another was just something that commonly happened, something accepted by the church and certainly encouraged by church growth experts. Carl F. George, who has been director of the Fuller Institute of Evangelism and Church Growth, teaches this principle:

> Why do some churches grow even without being strongly evangelistic? The most common explanation, which fits many of the large metropolitan-area churches, is that some develop a gravitational pull on the unhappy, the disillusioned and the underutilized from other churches. . . . Whenever members responded to internal congregational troubles by looking elsewhere for a new church home, they tended to drift to one or more churches that had distinguished themselves as receptor sites. These would grow large as a result of recurring troubles in the feeder churches. . . . A marketing term called positioning can be applied to churches that purposely restructure their image in order to be more appealing. . . . A church can deliberately set out to situate itself to become seen as the most viable option for meeting the spiritual and social needs of whatever segment of the population God's Spirit prompts it to target.[9]

This concept of transfer growth taught aggressively as a church growth principle did not originate with George but with the founding father of the movement, Donald McGavran. His motivations, which center on quality of care, were expressed in this excerpt from a self-study course used at Fuller Seminary:

> During the past fifty years, most pastors in North America have leaned over backwards to avoid the charge of "sheep stealing." Partly as a result of this, about a hundred million Americans are nominal, marginal, or slightly lapsed Christians. What is now demanded is that every church seek to be a better church—to have more biblical teaching, warmer fellowship, more Christian love, more concern for social justice, and more effective evangelism of the lost. When a prospect says, "I belong to another church," he

ought to be asked in as kindly a way as possible, "Are you a practicing Christian?" If the answers to these questions are not satisfactory, he (a sheep running wild on the range) ought to be found and folded, fed and transformed. If this be sheep stealing, let us steal boldly![10]

In the *Pastor's Church Growth Handbook*, McGavran envisions sheep stealing as a way to *rescue* sheep when they are being victimized by bad shepherds who demonstrate abusive tendencies. Sheep in these situations, McGavran would assert, need and deserve to be delivered. He tells this story to illustrate his concept of justifiable transfer growth:

> In Allahabad, India, about four miles from the city center, a suburb had developed at Naini. In it lived fourteen people who belonged to the downtown Church of North India. They almost never went to church or saw their pastor. Then in Naini, the Evangelical Church of India (a small denomination) started two new congregations which took in these fourteen and others. The downtown church angrily charged sheep stealing. To which the pastor of the Evangelical Church serenely replied, "Splendid! You go on sleeping and we'll go on stealing."[11]

Wagner, McGavran's understudy, develops a scriptural basis for transfer growth due to neglect that has exacerbated the tensions between traditional and church growth communities. Wagner likens traditional churches to the "bad shepherds" condemned in a biblical admonition to Israel in the book of Ezekiel[12]:

> The word of the LORD came to me: "Son of man, prophesy against the shepherds of Israel; prophesy and say to them: 'This is what the Sovereign LORD says: Woe to the shepherds of Israel who only take care of themselves! Should not shepherds take care of the flock? . . .
> "'Therefore, O shepherds, hear the word of the LORD: This is what the Sovereign LORD says: I am against the shepherds and will hold them accountable for my flock. I will remove them from tending the flock so that the shepherds can no longer feed themselves. I will rescue my flock from their mouths, and it will no longer be food for them.'" (Ezek 34:1-2, 9-10)

Church growth focuses on meeting the needs of the sheep, and that has commonly been the least important issue for many traditional churches, as they have appeared fixated on smallness. Writes David Wells:

> Smallness is presented by Church Growth advocates as a frame of mind, a condition resulting from an inability to think beyond the traditional, an inability to make connections with contemporary people, an inability to update routines, music, plans, expectations, services. Smallness is attributed to hidebound, pinched, and narrow thinking.[13]

Wagner asserts:

> Well-fed sheep cannot be stolen. When I go into a vital, living, growing church and talk to the lay people in that church and say why are you in that church, . . . they have no idea of leaving at all, they love their church, . . . and the pastors of those churches are not threatened by sheep stealing one iota. In fact the pastors of those churches usually say, "Look, if there is somebody in my church that's going to be happier in another church, they should go to that church, I don't want them around here." . . . The ones that are left are committed. Why are they committed? They are growing, their needs are being met, they are being fed.[14]

Clearly at this point the church growth experts not only endorse transfer growth but also imply that the grave biblical admonitions of Ezekiel 34 are appropriately directed at churches that refuse to become modernized to meet the needs of people in a variety of ministry and worship contexts. They advocate an ecclesiastical food chain in which the bigger church feeds on smaller ministries that are less adept at survival.

This aggressive raiding of other ministries, along with prophetic denunciations, has led to the drawing of a line between what the church used to endure and view as a natural process of transfer growth and what is now being identified as foul play. As the church growth movement's popularity rose, so did resentment toward the movement and concerns that biblical principles were being violated, and that modernization itself was a bastion of potential evils.

Our church, too, was guilty of eliciting resentment in our town. The growth masked the sin of tearing apart another church body as important members transferred their allegiance. As we prospered other churches languished and died. My peers in ministry were experiencing pressure to keep up with our church's programming, or lose their church families. It was pressure that I was putting on them leveraging my talents and education to exploit their weakness.

My focus was on our church and the fact that our church was growing indicated to me that we were pleasing the Lord. Our success blinded me to the shallowness of such growth, or the addictiveness of all the comparative accolades. One rarely perceives evil when one is profiting from it.

In church growth, bigger is better because size empowers you to generate the resources you need to achieve new expansion programs "for the kingdom."[15] I never considered the devastating effects that sheep stealing could have on a church when the people began to leave the flock for greener pastures. Future events would change all of that.

Within a couple of years an interesting phenomenon began to emerge: the foundations of *our* church began to crack. All the exciting growth had brought with it a host of unification and support issues.

I discovered, to my surprise, that when issues arose calling for spiritual disciplines of forgiveness, holiness and commitment, many of our parishioners began looking for fellowship that was less demanding. They did not want to deal with what I consider spiritual maturity growth, such as learning how to live together in unity. They rebelled against such personal challenges and left the church.

A negative flow began to drain the life's blood out of the church. Those who had come to our church searching for "more of the Spirit" or "better worship" or "biblical preaching" were taking off in search of their elusive quarry once again. I became embattled on a multitude of ill-defined fronts as the sheep panicked.

Suffice it to say that Satan dined as the flock scattered. What had been a dynamic church growth setting was now a broken shell of a church, and I was left discouraged, hurt and confused. I begged God to release me from my pastoral vow—I was ready to seek some other kind of work.

All That Glitters

In this context I began considering the effects of some church growth practices that had initially helped us to expand so rapidly. In the sober moments of a failed ministry I began to acknowledge that the Lord does use defeat and hardship as tools to train us in his ways, and my earnest heart's cry was to understand this harsh pruning process.

Was I being disciplined? If so, then for what purpose? For the author of Hebrews promises that "no discipline seems pleasant at the time, but painful. Later on, however, it produces a harvest of righteousness and peace for those who have been trained by it" (Heb 12:11). Don Baker writes in *Beyond Forgiveness:*

> God's children must and do experience chastisement. Chastisement is the necessary and inevitable child training process that, in its extreme, can take on the form of "scourgings"—physical pain—or can come as gentile, mild, whispered reminders of God's wishes to the minds of His children. Chastisement can be corrective and it can be preventative. Job's chastisement was for the purpose of revealing Jehovah God to the world, God to Job, and Job to himself. Abraham's chastisement was simply for the development of spiritual graces in his life. Paul was chastised, not for his sin, but to prevent him from becoming proud. David experienced the severe blows of God's chastening rod for his open wickedness. Chastening is designed for perfecting.[16]

If you have suffered the humiliation of a church split, you know the depth of nights filled with agonizing prayer, waves of utter despair, depression and loneliness. God dealt with my own heart, character and ministry, and he also exposed the wrongness of certain practices that had led to the demise of our church and ultimately undermined the health of Christ's body.

Growth for the sake of growth is wrong. *How* a church grows matters—especially when basic biblical principles are being compromised to achieve the success.

The Truth Is

Biblical church growth involves the addition of new believers, as in the early church: "And the Lord added to their number daily those who were being saved" (Acts 2:47).

Transfer growth, by definition, creates no numerical growth in the kingdom of God. In fact the term is an oxymoron, and grossly misleading, for its net result is simply much ado about nothing. There are no new converts, no baptisms, no expansion of knowledge of God in the world, and no salvation fruit from this labor. Arguably—and contrary to popular belief—there is no known purely positive kingdom benefit from a membership change!

Wagner, one of the founding fathers of the modern church growth movement and a leading expert on church growth, continues to make this very point: "Transfer growth is the increase of certain congregations at the expense of others; members go from one church to another."[17] Dubbed by one set of authors the "Circulation of the Saints," this process has less to do with the natural growth of the body of Christ than with the intrinsic evils that come with the building of personal church empires.

Here we begin to discover the central problem with transfer growth. Its orientation is not the good of God's kingdom but the prosperity of one individual or church.[18] So although a ministry is growing and attracting new people, it may not actually be evangelizing. If the service includes an excellent greeting time but the church is filled with folks who have walked away from relationships because of unresolved pain, we are mocking agape love. Are we truly making disciples of Jesus Christ, or are we violating biblical principles?

> Do nothing out of selfish ambition or vain conceit, but in humility
> consider others better than yourselves. Each of you should look not
> only to your own interests, but also to the interests of others.
> Your attitude should be the same as that of Christ Jesus:
> Who, being in very nature God,
>   did not consider equality with God something to be grasped,
> but made himself nothing,
>   taking the very nature of a servant,
>   being made in human likeness.
> And being found in appearance as a man,
>   he humbled himself
>   and became obedient to death—even death on a cross!
> Therefore God exalted him to the highest place
>   and gave him the name that is above every name,
> that at the name of Jesus every knee should bow,
>   in heaven and on earth and under the earth,
> and every tongue confess that Jesus Christ is Lord,
>   to the glory of God the Father. (Phil 2:3-11)

The primary principle was one I had been taught years earlier; it had to do with bubblegum, bottles and Mom. Stealing motivated by ambition, even for the sake of growing churches, is wrong, and no good end will come of it. The longer I examined the phenomenon of transfer growth, the more it became clear that this practice is energized not by God's Spirit but by God's enemy.

2

Bleating Sheep

When Samuel reached him, Saul said,
"The LORD bless you! I have carried out the LORD's instructions."
But Samuel said, "What then is this bleating of sheep
in my ears?" 1 SAMUEL 15:13-14

A sin—no way sheep stealing is a sin! I pastor a church of four thousand people in Dallas, Texas. If what you are proposing is true, then you have totally condemned much of the growth we have experienced in the last three years," lamented one pastor.

"You cannot call it stealing," suggested another clergyman, "People in Colorado are independent. They church hop all the time. There is nothing we can do about that; it's a way of life."

"Well, if what we offer is better, then people should be able to come to our church," argued a third. "It keeps churches sharp and weeds out the dead ones. In my opinion, if you are not meeting the needs of your congregation, then you are just begging for a better church to steal your flock."

These were three colleagues' immediate responses to my doctoral thesis on transfer growth. The transferring of members from one church to another has been a common source of many churches' growth for years. Few pastors are willing to walk away from the practice. Fewer still are willing to confront the issue. Almost none will entertain the notion that they are not pleasing God when their churches engage extensively in sheep stealing.

Bleating sheep is a powerful biblical image of being caught red-handed in the midst of profiteering. Saul was reinterpreting the instructions of the Lord in a vain attempt to appease God while capitalizing on personal and corporate opportunities for social and economic gain.

Transfer growth attempts to straddle a similar fence. All church growth seems God-pleasing, because it appears to be expanding God's work and kingdom. But when our church growth involves massive membership transfers, we need to ask who that growth's true beneficiary is.

For my colleagues, a key objection to questioning the ethics of transfer growth stemmed from my use of the word *stealing*. Clearly, stealing in any form is not God's will. "Thou shalt not steal" is one of God's charter commandments in the Decalogue (see Ex 20:15). But as my upset colleagues were eager to point out, people are not really sheep, or property, so to view them as something that can be stolen seems off base.

This is a legitimate objection to equating transfer growth with stealing. Can people be viewed as actually *belonging to* a particular church? When you join a church do you become an actual part of that church body such that leaving it becomes a spiritual violation?

These are not easy questions to answer. Many would argue that the catholicity of the church is key to the issue. When we become disciples of Christ, we join the *church universal:* spiritual in dimension, worldwide in geographic scope, multidenominational in character. Christians—especially Protestants—frequently say their allegiance and responsibility belong solely to Christ. So if they move around a bit from church to church but remain faithful to the Lord, can the concept of stealing really be applied?

What Is the Church?

Use of the term *stealing* becomes more appropriate as we carefully consider the functional nature of the church. When we understand the genius of the body of Christ and the importance of relationships within it, we begin to grasp the important role of membership fidelity in maturing and prospering the church.

Ironically, church growth literature has been remiss in defining the term *church*. The church, it would appear, is suffering from an identity crisis. Of the forty volumes on church growth in my own library, none had a chapter dealing with this subject. There are many chapters on how to change the image of a church, or how to grow a church, or what the church's biblical mission is, but somehow defining the church itself has been overlooked.

"Only once in thirty-four years of publication has the Evangelical Theological Society addressed the doctrine of the church."[1] *Leadership, Christianity Today* and *Charisma* have done no better. The topic of defining the church seems to have been ignored, perhaps because of an assumption that everyone knows what the church is. That simply is not the case.

A building? One definition of the church I remember from a little child's rhyme acted out with hand movements. "Here is the church [forming a square with the hands]; here is the steeple [forming a triangle with the index fingers]; open the doors [thumbs swing back]; and see all the people [fingers interlocked to suggest wiggly bodies in the building]." As a little boy, I assumed a church is a building. Sometimes called "edifice complex," this is a popular and dominant definition of the church.

"No perception," writes Charles Colson, "is more firmly rooted in our culture than that the Church is a building—a view held by both the churched and the unchurched alike." The concept is readily expressed in our everyday dialogue. "Who does not say, 'I am going to church?' We call the place where we worship, the church. And when we say, 'we are building a church' we mean we are constructing a facility. . . . In ten thousand common expres-

36   Stealing Sheep

sions we refer to the church as a place."[2]

Commitment to a building does not mean much to people who move an average of once every five years. If a person's perception of church is that it is a facility, it is easy to see why there is little remorse when people change churches. Such a low view of the church gives no particular reason to consider the impact of transferring membership.

The people? A second common perception is that the church is *people* who gather. Charles Van Engen tells this story: "The class roared with laughter. But the tall, solemn African pastor declared that he had not been joking; 'Brother Chuck, you asked what is the least we would need to still have the church? I am serious when I say all I need is a bell. I can walk out into the bush in my country, stand under a tree, begin ringing the bell, and the church gathers.'"[3]

This perception of the church is closer to the biblical understanding of the church. However, often an important aspect of this definition is not clarified: *what people?* Many view the church as a social club. They join the church in the same way they join a country club, Kiwanis, Rotary or the Masons.

This view downplays the significance of the church's importance in a person's life. It is there only to provide status, programming and services such as weddings and funerals. Changing churches thus has to do with keeping up with the Joneses or upholding ethnic and cultural norms rather than expressing some sort of organic relationship. When the church is viewed in this fashion, church loyalty is commonly expressed by attendance only at Christmastime or Easter.

A denomination? Which is the true Christian church, the building or the people—or is it a denomination that holds the right to the title "the church"? Millions of Protestant, Orthodox and Roman Catholics parishioners view the true church as their particular faith and teachings.

Recently in the northeast United States there has been an overt effort by the Catholic Church to win back the thousands of mem-

bers who have stopped attending Mass or who have abandoned
their faith and joined Protestant churches. Utilizing radio advertise-
ments and colorful banners on the sides of their church buildings,
they have aggressively attempted to woo back lapsed members. A
pamphlet distributed by Catholics during a Luis Palau evangelistic
crusade in Portland, Maine, stated boldly, "The Holy Roman Catholic Church is the only true church. To be a true disciple of the Lord
Jesus Christ is to be Catholic."

Foundational to this view is the concept that the pope as the
bishop of Rome is the one true heir to the apostolic authority given
by Christ to Peter (Mt 16:18). The pope "is considered the man on
earth who represents the Son of God, who takes the place of the
Second Person of the omnipotent God of the Trinity."[4]

According to Jesuit thinker Robert Bellarmine (d. 1621), then,
"the one and true Church [is] the community of men brought
together by the profession of the same Christian Faith and con-
joined in the communion of the same sacraments, under the gov-
ernment of the legitimate pastors and especially the one vicar of
Christ on earth, the Roman pontiff."[5] Any so-called church that
does not fall under the pope's authority is, from a Roman Catholic
perspective, no church at all.

All the above? A host of organizations claim to be "the church."
The American Internal Revenue Service struggles with defining the
term, as many groups and individuals seek the tax advantages that
come from having religious status. Liberally applied to a variety of
movements, the term *church* has become a catchall phrase,
encompassing cults, religious organizations, tax dodgers and militant social factions.

The biblical model. In the New Testament the term *ekklēsia*
("church" or "assembly," literally "the called-out ones") appears
some 111 times. Seventy-three times it is specifically referring to
the gathering of people,[6] but never does it refer to a building (the
Eph 2:19-22 use of the term is metaphorical) or a specific denomination. The *ekklēsia* is a gathering of the people of God (saints) or,

as Carl Henry refers to them, "the new society of God's people, the new society of the twice-born."[7]

Being twice born is the distinguishing characteristic of the true church, or the called-out (from the world) *gathering* of God. All of humankind has experienced physical birth, but the church is distinguished by the experience of a second birth, a spiritual birth. Commonly referred to as becoming born again (see Jn 3:3; 1 Pet 1:23; 1 Jn 3:9), the spiritual birth is facilitated by a personal confession of sin, reception of Jesus Christ as one's Lord and Savior (Rom 10:9-10) and infilling of God's Spirit (Eph 1:13), and it is demonstrated through a life of obedience to God (1 Jn 3:6). The church, those who are born again, is found in all denominations and cultural settings; corporately the church is corporately God's children (1 Pet 2:9-10), the church universal.

The Church Universal

Every believer in Jesus Christ holds a membership in the church universal. This confession is found in the earliest creeds of the church: "I believe in one holy, catholic and apostolic Church; I acknowledge one baptism for the remission of sins. I await the resurrection of the dead and the life of the ages to come"[8] (see Eph 4:4-6).

The church universal transcends time and space to include those who have died in Christ and await the arrival of his kingdom (the church triumphal) and those who are alive and working on the earth today (the church militant; see 1 Thess 4:13-17). Both comprise the church universal, but it is the militant aspect that provides for us the image of the church that is most commonly portrayed in the New Testament—physical gatherings of believers who join together in an effort to grow in their faith and spread the gospel. Dr. Charles Van Engen makes this helpful distinction: "There is the church that God purchased with the blood of Jesus and called to be his people in the world [universal]," and "there is the church, that congregation of believers in fellowship who seek God's purposes [militant]."[9]

The House Church

The church as *a congregation* of believers in fellowship is first portrayed in the book of Acts.

> When those moved by Peter's powerful sermon [at Pentecost] asked what they should do, the apostle replied, "Repent and be baptized," . . . and [they] would be among those whom the Lord called to Himself—that is the Church [universal]. . . . Then they gathered together for the apostles' teaching, fellowship, breaking of bread, and prayer (the church congregation).[10]

Colson notes, "Immediately after Pentecost, [Jesus] established the pattern: Individual believers were to gather into particular communities."[11]

This pattern of establishing house churches or assemblies of believers dominates the New Testament. The apostle Paul specialized in founding these churches (Acts 16:15, Philippi; Acts 17:3, Thessalonica; Acts 18:7, Corinth), providing a governing system for them (1 Tim 3:1-13) and serving them (2 Tim 4:6). The genius of the early church movement was the excellent care and oversight the churches provided to the early converts to the faith (Acts 2:42; 6:1-6). This, combined with the flexibility of the assembly model, enabled the gospel to spread at an unprecedented rate, until Christianity became the state religion of the entire Roman Empire.

It makes sense, then, to define the church as having two natures: the church universal, encompassing all believers, and the local church congregation. It is in the church as a congregation that the dynamics of a person's spiritual giftedness develop into fruitfulness.

The Genius of the Body

In *Images of the Church in the New Testament* Paul Minear looks at ninety-six word images used to make vivid the church's nature. One single image demands an entire chapter because it pictures how the church functions both vertically in relationship to the Lord and horizontally in relationship to each other: the church as the *body of Christ*.[12]

Four primary characteristics of the church are highlighted by the metaphor of the body. First, Christ is the head of the body (Col 1:18). Second, the body has many parts (1 Cor 12:14). Third, all of these parts are vital to the success of the body (1 Cor 12:22). Fourth, the body is the church (1 Cor 12:27-31). Examining these four characteristics will help us identify key components that are essential in the development of personal spirituality and divine mission.

The Head

To say that Christ is the head of the body is to declare God's sovereignty over the body: "And he is the head of the body, the church; he is the beginning and the firstborn from among the dead, so that in everything he might have the supremacy" (Col 1:18).

There is an ironic twist to the freedom in Christ that is often used as an excuse for church hopping. The Bible teaches that human beings share one trait: all people are slaves to sin (Rom 6:17). Freedom implies that somehow we have been liberated from our previous position as slaves to sin and death. This was accomplished through the death of Christ, who paid for our sins (again, Rom 6:17). Paul goes on to argue that legally we have become the property of God. We have been bought with a price; thus we are not our own (1 Cor 6:20) but the property of him who saved us. Our freedom is totally subject to God's sovereignty.

It is not unreasonable to assume, then, that Christ, the head of the church, might have a plan and a mission for each person he has purchased to be in his kingdom. I am implying that the body has been *carefully* arranged. Divine appointment, if you will, goes into the development of each church, each part of the body.

God's very nature supports the logic of this argument. The God who created the universe with balance and symmetry (Ps 19:1) is also the God who calls to himself in a million different settings those he has ordained to be a part of his church, universal and particular. It is his right, for he owns us, and it is his nature to lay with deliberate precision the living stones of his temple (1 Pet 2:5).

It was not happenstance that selected the members of the Twelve. "Jesus went up on a mountainside [and spent the night praying to God—Lk 6:12] and called to him those he wanted, and they came to him. He appointed twelve—designating them apostles" (Mk 3:13-14). Christ carefully considered and chose each one of them, even the son of perdition (Jn 17:12 KJV).

Was Paul an accident (Acts 26:17)? Were Lydia, Epenetus, Junias, Apollos and the other critical players in the early church converted by luck so that the work of the kingdom would flourish? Rather, we see over and over again in the New Testament that the evangel is presented so that the "elect" might hear the gospel and respond (1 Pet 1:1).

The body of Christ is a product of the sovereign Lord. It is fearfully and wonderfully made. Each facet of this body, each component of the whole, is celebrated, for it was chosen by the Master Builder to fit perfectly into its spot. As surely as God spoke these words to Jeremiah, "Before I formed you in the womb I knew you, before you were born I set you apart; I appointed you as a prophet to the nations" (Jer 1:5), so God has orchestrated the development of his church and each individual in it.

God's motivation for this development of his church is that same motivation that brought him to the earth in advent love. Each person is given a gift (1 Cor 12:7) to be used as a formative piece of the development of the body. That means each person is uniquely designed, custom fit to the body of which she or he becomes a part. Each member is loved and valued, and each church is properly equipped for the task of bringing the Lord's love to a lost and dying world (Jn 3:16).

Transfer growth is in essence, I believe, an act of rebellion against the sovereignty of God. What would the church of Christ look like if all its members had bloomed where they were planted?

Would the church be far more efficient? Would it be better endowed? Would it be healthier, with giftedness spread throughout its ranks, instead of the cream of the crop concentrating in a few "hot" churches?

At the 1976 Urbana missions convention Luis Palau bellowed, "Missionaries are a lot like cow manure. If you pile them all up in one spot, they stink. But if you spread them around a little bit, they can do a lot of good!" Perhaps this is how we are supposed to function in the body of Christ: to develop where we are and, in so doing, be a part of raising the standards and faith of those around us. "From him the whole body, joined and held together by every supporting ligament, grows and builds itself up in love, as each part does its work" (Eph 4:16).

Hands and Feet

The second characteristic of the New Testament church is that it is composed of *many different parts.* "Now the body is not made up of one part but of many. . . . God has arranged the parts in the body, every one of them, just as he wanted them to be . . . so that there should be no division in the body, but that its parts should have equal concern for each other" (1 Cor 12:14, 18, 25).

To coexist with individuals who are different from us is not our natural inclination. The movie *Remember the Titans* portrays the true story of a football coach who attempts to overcome segregation on the gridiron. Conflicts abound as white Southern boys struggle to develop relationships with their black counterparts. Many times those on both sides are ready to give up the effort, but through unity of mission and love the team forges a union, becoming state champions.

That's Hollywood. In the church diversity is often a catalyst for conflict that results in copious amounts of transfer growth! The apostle Paul learned about the importance of diversity in the body the hard way. Acts 15:36-41 tells how, preparing to launch out on his second missionary tour, Paul was confronted by his mentor

Barnabas about the need to bring along a young man named John Mark. Paul would not hear of it. John Mark had been on the first tour but deserted the company when Paul had decided to travel on to Perga and Pamphylia (Acts 13:13). Although the reasons for John Mark's desertion are not recorded, it is speculated that he may have been uncomfortable with the prospect of allowing Gentiles to hear the message of Christ.

Returning to Jerusalem, John Mark may have contributed to the controversy that was brewing within the church over the issue of Gentile conversions (Acts 15). Paul and Barnabas appeared before that assembly of the apostles and had to defend their evangelistic efforts. They recounted many stories of how Gentiles' conversions had been validated as the Spirit of God was pleased to make his home in them (Acts 15:12). In the end, they won the right to keep on advancing the gospel into Asia Minor, but Paul was left with little respect for a part of the body that had almost succeeded in thwarting his mission.

So angry was Paul with John Mark that he severed relationship with his best friend Barnabas over the issue of bringing the younger man on their journey. "They had such a sharp disagreement that they parted company. Barnabas took Mark and sailed for Cyprus, but Paul chose Silas and left" (Acts 15:39-40).

It is our natural inclination to desire to be surrounded with like-minded people. All the great cities of the world include neighborhoods divided by ethnic and social stratification. Even the Christian church is full of struggles between groups or factions that may have the same goals but are separated by age, preferred methods or membership seniority.

"They are driving me crazy," a young pastor confided. "I accepted a call to this church because they wanted to attract young families. Well, now the young families are here, and all I hear is complaints how the new people are taking over. 'They're not doing things the way we do them.' 'All they want is change. What's wrong with the old way of running the church?' Three of the char-

ter members of the church, people who were on my search committee, just placed an envelope on my desk and said that if I didn't
fix things by Sunday, I could open up the envelope and read their
resignations to the church!"

"The eye cannot say to the hand, 'I don't need you!' And the
head cannot say to the feet, 'I don't need you!' On the contrary,
those parts of the body that seem to be weaker are indispensable"
(1 Cor 12:21-22). In the church, "indispensable" means that everyone is needed, each person has value. When we approach ministry
with that in mind, we discover that God does not make mistakes.
We are together for a reason, and our mission for God requires the
whole team.

It would be years before the apostle Paul fully understood that
God created diversity to empower unity. Not only does diversity
stretch us, causing us to grow in the Lord's grace and experience
his wisdom, but it prods to develop the gift of love, that defining
characteristic of Christ and his church (Jn 13:35).

In the last letter Paul wrote we read, "Get Mark and bring him
with you, because he is helpful to me in my ministry" (2 Tim 4:11).
These words reflect the heart of a man who had learned a key lesson about the body of Christ. John Mark, though different from
Paul, was indispensable. Cutting him out of Paul's world had
allowed sin to mock God's design for the church. Even the greatly
gifted Paul had to realize that all the parts of the body really are
indispensable.

It is satanic when we say that we must leave a church because
of some difference with another part of the body. It mocks forgiveness, it mocks reconciliation, and it mocks the new life we are supposed to have in Christ. Transferring out of a church in conflict
reflects the worst in our sinful nature and denies the significance of
Christ's death on the cross.

> Do not be deceived: God cannot be mocked. A man reaps what he
> sows. The one who sows to please his sinful nature, from that
> nature will reap destruction; the one who sows to please the Spirit,

from the Spirit will reap eternal life. Let us not become weary in
doing good . . . especially to those who belong to the family of
believers. (Gal 6:7-10)

Love is the standard. Although we are different, the body is *supposed* to be made up of many parts. When we understand the
genius of the body, we will grow to appreciate the fact that like-mindedness allows a very limited scope for growth and outreach.

"He told me that his son was gay and that he had to leave the
church because he knew that the church body would condemn his
child," a fellow pastor told me. "I was sickened by his accurate
portrayal of evangelical Christianity. We would not share each
other's burdens or weep when he was weeping. No, rejection
would surely occur. In a thousand different ways, in a hundred different glances, this part of the body would be cut off.

"At that moment that I realized that I needed this man more
than ever in my life. We needed to walk this path together, iron
sharpening iron, as we struggled to apply our faith in a real world.
Paul said, 'If one part of the body suffers, every part suffers with it;
if one part is honored, every part rejoices with it' [1 Cor 12:26]. I
suddenly understood that commitment and love would be the only
places where this family would have a chance of experiencing the
healing touch of Jesus Christ. Anything less I realized would be
short of the love of God, short of what he would expect from his
church."

Such commitment to the body, generated by the love that Jesus
says will mark his disciples, fosters true spiritual maturity. Spiritual
growth requires a process of protecting one another.

The natural body is very committed to its parts! The eyelid will
blink to protect the eye, the hand will jet out to break a fall, the
stomach will tense up to protect the other internal organs. Because
of their inseparable nature, all the parts of the body have a vested
interest in each other's well-being. They strive to maintain the
highest quality of life in each part for the common good.

This is the level of commitment that the apostle Paul had in mind when he wrote in Ephesians 4:11-13: "It was he who gave some to be apostles, some to be prophets, some to be evangelists, and some to be pastors and teachers, to prepare God's people for works of service, so that the body of Christ may be built up until we all reach unity in the faith and in the knowledge of the Son of God and become mature, attaining to the whole measure of the fullness of Christ."

Who Is Thaddaeus?

Minear's third defining principle of the church is that the various parts of the body are vital to its success. When Paul writes that "God has combined the members of the body" (1 Cor 12:24), he is implying that the sovereign Head, creator of the many parts, does not have leftover pieces scattered about the floor when he completes his church. All the members are essential for the success of the church.

Our class roared with laughter as Professor Dick Peace went down the eclectic list of the apostles. James and John seemed like terrible candidates for apostleship, lusting after power (Mk 10:35) and calling down fire on unbelievers' heads (Lk 9:54). Matthew the tax collector could not have been a worse choice. Despised by all Jews, this man of low status would surely undermine the group's success (Mk 2:14). Simon the Zealot (Lk 6:15), assassin of friends of the Romans, could not wait to get Matthew in a dark alley. And then there was Thaddaeus. Who the heck is Thaddaeus? Commanding only two references in the entire Bible (Mt 10:3; Mk 3:18), this individual was nevertheless chosen to be part of Christ's elite first assembly of believers.

"Thaddaeus," suggested Peace, "is there for the rest of us. He may well have been just average. He certainly did not stand out in any mission endeavor, yet there he is—chosen. It is as if God were saying to us all, everybody counts."

Paul never would have guessed that the young man he was so disappointed with had a unique and valuable mission to complete for the body of Christ. Years after the old apostle died, John Mark gave the church an invaluable gift when he wrote the first recorded (A.D. 70?) account of the life and times of Jesus the Christ. The book of Mark became the standard from which two other Gospel writers would fashion their accounts. Had Mark been permanently rejected by Paul and cut off from the church, how much poorer we would all be!

When we submit to the sovereignty of Christ as the head of the church and grasp the fact that the body is composed of many different parts, we can begin to appreciate the different ways God made us. Each part is vital for the success of the church of Jesus Christ.

The Church Is the Body of Christ

The church body is the presence of Christ on the earth today, and we are called to be active parts of it. "Now you are the body of Christ, and each one of you is a part of it" (1 Cor 12:27). This is a declarative statement. Membership is not optional. If you are in Christ, you should be a part of his body (universal) and a committed member of a congregation of believers (local). As each church is an interdependent assembly of its many parts, you are needed, and you need others to experience life in Christ.

Failure to be a part of the church is inappropriate for a believer. "And let us consider how we may spur one another on toward love and good deeds. Let us not give up meeting together, as some are in the habit of doing, but let us encourage one another—and all the more as you see the Day approaching" (Heb 10:24-25).

In the account of God's creation of Adam, one interesting part of his character quickly comes into focus: "It is not good for the man to be alone. I will make a helper suitable for him" (Gen 2:18). This helper (Hebrew *'ezer,* used to designate divine aid)[13] was commissioned to carry out the creation mandate with the man.

So God created man in his own image, in the image of God he created him; male and female he created them.

> God blessed them and said to them, "Be fruitful and increase in
> number; fill the earth and subdue it. Rule over the fish of the sea
> and the birds of the air and over every living creature that moves on
> the ground." (Gen. 1:27-28)

The creation mandate shows that God did not intend any individual to do the work of the Lord alone. We simply were never made to function outside of the matrix of interdependency. We need God and we need one another.

Perhaps that's why the Lord insists on colaboring in the ministry of prayer. "I tell you that if two of you on earth agree about anything you ask for, it will be done for you by my Father in heaven. For where two or three come together in my name, there am I with them" (Mt 18:19-20). When Jesus commissioned the apostles, he sent them out two by two (Mk 6:7). There is a need for the spiritual integrity that two bring to the task; one is inherently incapable of producing it. Our mandate to serve God has continued to require plurality since creation.

Terry Fullam of St. Paul's Episcopal Church in Darien, Connecticut, struggled to teach his church the need for mutual interdependency in ministry. *Miracle in Darien* records these words that he spoke to his vestry arguing this point: "You see, the Holy Spirit has been given to us for the express purpose of leading us into a knowledge of what the will of God is. But He won't lead only one person. That's the thing we have to grasp, you see. He's not going to lead just one person in the church and show him what's the right thing to do. His plan is to lead the whole group."[14]

In the book of Acts the functionality of this interdependence is well established as Luke records the formative years of the early church. The selection of Matthias (Acts 1:21), the formation of the fellowship of believers (Acts 2:42), the meeting of corporate needs (Acts 6:1), the definition of evangelistic outreach (Acts 8), the commissioning for missionary endeavors (Acts 13), the defining of church doctrine (Acts 15) and the structure of new ministries (Acts 16-19) all bear the mark of corporate involvement as the standard for kingdom development.

In the epistles Paul is highly committed to the spiritual aspects of interdependence. He was quick to quell rebellions of spiritual independence (1 Cor 3) which were divisive to the body, and through the Holy Spirit he was given a remarkable image of interdependence: the church as the incarnate body of Christ in the world today (Rom 12; 1 Cor 12; Eph 4).

Radical Individualism Confronts the Church

Failing to understand what the church is, to value the diversity of the body of Christ, to grasp the strength of unity in mission, to invest in love as the bond of peace has created an isolationist mentality among denominations, churches and individuals. Such isolationism feeds the fires of transfer growth.

"I am my own church," responded one person to a Gallup poll on the church. With this mindset comes behavior based solely on personal gratification and personal values. This isolationism is killing the church. What sociologist Robert Bellah has called "radical individualism"[15] the mentality of "Jesus and me" has replaced the extended spiritual family that made up the early church of the New Testament. Radical individualism fails to see the value in others and has no problem with disassociating from them.

When I became a Christian, my salvation experience had been twofold. I felt that when I was led to Christ I was not only saved from sin and death but also from a religious institution that had failed to show me how to find God. I resented the church for being an irresponsible guardian of my soul, and I made that point to my priest when I sat down to tell him about my recent conversion.

In college I was wonderfully discipled by an InterVarsity staff member named David Montague who exposed me to the vital ministries of parachurch organizations. These independent ministries appeared to me to arise from the churches' inadequacies. With their focus on evangelism and relational discipleship, para-

church organizations seemed filled with passion, life and individual freedom to be about doing great things for God.

By the time I graduated from seminary in the early 1980s, I was
suffering from radical individualism. As I began my career in professional ministry, my experience with denominations and
churches was very discouraging. My naiveté about church politics,
rules and systems stymied my attempts to engage in ministry with
the same freedom and at the same levels that I had enjoyed in
parachurch organizations.

The church quickly began to represent a hindrance to the
spread of Christianity, instead of the keeper of the flame. Even as a
pastor I had a low regard for the institution and struggled with valuing all of its members. At best I viewed the church as a necessary
evil created by Christ for reasons that were beyond my grasp.

The success of my service to Christ's gospel, I erroneously
believed, rested entirely on my relationship with the Lord and the
personal insights he gave me. Others simply watered down decision-making and slowed me down. Sadly, years passed before I
began to understand and appreciate the genius behind the creation
of the body of Christ.[16]

A Case for Body Life

The church was never designed to operate with radical individualism as a primary building block. A survey of the many models of
spiritual governance available in the Old and New Testaments
shows clearly that radical individualism was not chosen by Christ
as a model for ministry.

A failed attempt to apply radical individualism in ministry
appears in Exodus 18. Here we see Moses attempting to govern
God's people as the sole agent of all decisions and divine declara-
tions. His work of regulating the affairs of a million-plus people
quickly led to disenchantment, conflict and confusion. Working
from dawn to dusk (Ex 18:13), Moses was simply exhausted.

I suspect that his wife complained to her mother about the horrible hours her husband was keeping. Moses' mother-in-law, in turn, was likely the one to put the bug in her husband's ear to speak with Moses. Then, guided by the Holy Spirit, Jethro gave these directives to Moses for how the Lord wanted his people governed:

> The work is too heavy for you. . . . Teach [the people] the decrees and laws, and show them the way to live and the duties they are to perform. But select capable men from all the people—men who fear God, trustworthy men who hate dishonest gain—and appoint them as officials over thousands, hundreds, fifties and tens. . . . That will make your load lighter, because they will share it with you. If you do this and God so commands, you will be able to stand the strain, and all these people will go home satisfied. (Ex 18:18, 20-23)

Unfortunately, this concept of sharing the load of the work of the church and valuing the Holy Spirit's skills in other people does not come naturally to fallen human beings. It was not long in the history of God's people before another model of governance was adopted, to Israel's utter detriment.

In 1 Samuel 8 the elders of the nation of Israel revert to an autocratic form of governance: "Give us a king to lead us. . . . We want a king over us. Then we will be like all the other nations, with a king to lead us and to go out before us and fight our battles" (1 Sam 8:6, 19-20). Despite Samuel's warnings, Israel insistently devalued the divine injunction to govern through the strength of the Holy Spirit in the people and reverted to a singular dependency on an individual.

The Choice of Christ

Once Jesus' public ministry began, he took little time before establishing the form of governance he would use to build his church. "Jesus went up on a mountainside and called to him those he wanted, and they came to him. He appointed twelve—designating them apostles—that they might be with him and that he might send them out to preach and to have authority to drive out demons" (Mk 3:13-15). Thus Jesus follows the outline of governance that God had given to Moses through Jethro for leading the nation of Israel. Christ chose the value of the body over radical individualism.

Several times radical individualism is confronted in the Gospels.

"Teacher," [James and John] said, "we want you to do for us whatever we ask."

"What do you want me to do for you?" he asked.

They replied, "Let one of us sit at your right and the other at your left in your glory" (Mk 10:35-37)

James and John were eager to grab positions of control in Christ's kingdom, to promote self and foster the agenda of one as opposed to the agenda of the body.

Christ's rebuke was swift: "You know that those who are regarded as rulers of the Gentiles lord it over them, and their high officials exercise authority over them. Not so with you. Instead, whoever wants to become great among you must be your servant, and whoever wants to be first must be slave of all" (Mk 10:42-44). For Jesus leadership was found in excelling in body life. Upbuilding, serving and taking care of others through developing in them the skills to govern God's church were of primary importance.

Through the Years

That wildcat Christians might roam about doing the work of the Lord was foreign to the early church fathers. Indeed there were spiritual hermits and monks, but they had spiritual advisers who kept them accountable. St. Augustine wrote of the fallacy of faith without community: "He cannot have God for his father who does not have the church for his mother." For the early shapers of Christianity, community—being a committed part of a body—was the key and central ingredient to experiencing real Christian life.

The Reformers who broke away from the Catholic Church are often thought of as being models for radical individualism. Yet they held Christian community in very high regard. John Calvin made the point with conviction: "So highly does the Lord esteem the communion of His church that He considers everyone a traitor and apostate from religion who perversely withdraws himself from any Christian society which preserves the true ministry of the word and sacraments."[17]

Christian thinkers who write about the church today often reflect on the importance of community. Richard John Neuhaus, in his book *Freedom for Ministry,* is an example: "There is no Christianity apart from the historical community that bears its truth."[18]

Since the church is the body of Christ, each of us needs to understand and maintain our position in it. We were placed there with deliberate care and are a valuable part of the whole. To leave can be likened to the severing of a piece of your flesh: painful at any level, and lethal if critical parts are removed.

The Church and Unity

In *God's Missionary People* Charles Van Engen identifies four primary functions of the church. The first is to cultivate *unity* so that the church may gather to Jesus those who are his (Col 1:28), establish an organic cohesion (Eph 1:9-10), strive to become one (Jn 17) by the building up of the body (Eph 4:11-13), prepare for the Lord's return (Rev 19:7), and preserve the bond of peace (Eph 4:3).[18] "I would emphasize," writes Howard Snyder, "the priority of community in two directions: in relation to the individual believer and in relation to witness."[20]

Unity is all about love. "The gift and service of love was the manifestation of the pluriform unity of the members in the one body. The image of the body and the image of love should for all significant purposes be considered one image; they cannot, in fact, be considered otherwise, since the primary content of both is determined by the image of Christ."[21]

Love is the unifying agent that knits the body together (Col 2:2) and is the identifying characteristic of those who are in the body of Christ (1 Jn 4:7-8). Many commentators see it as no accident that 1 Corinthians 13, the love chapter, was placed between two chapters that describe the church as the body of Christ:

> First Corinthians, chapter 13, must therefore be interpreted as having major ecclesiological importance. . . . We must not fail to suggest that Paul intended this description of love as an exposition of the meaning of the one body (ch. 12) and the building up of the church (ch. 14). The works of love (ch. 13:4-7) were the primary means for enhancing the interdependence of the body's members. Consequently, this love defined what it meant to be the *soma*.[22]

The body needs commitment and fidelity to promote spiritual growth and to minister with spiritual power. Faith needs the safety net of commitment before a person can venture out on the wire of hope:

> "Lord, if it's you," Peter replied, "tell me to come to you on the water."
> "Come," he said.
> Then Peter got down out of the boat, walked on the water and came toward Jesus. But when he saw the wind, he was afraid and, beginning to sink, cried out, "Lord, save me!"
> Immediately Jesus reached out his hand and caught him. (Mt 14:28-31)

Unity and fidelity were central components of Jesus' teaching style. He purposely chose to disciple the apostles experientially (Mk 3:14) so that he could create an atmosphere of commitment in which the disciples could know him, trust him and in the end follow him. "That . . . which we have heard, which we have seen with our eyes, which we have looked at and our hands have touched—this we proclaim concerning the Word of life" (1 Jn 1:1). It was in knowing him that they discovered God.

Their discovery of God was not one-dimensional. They saw Jesus perform miracles yet be rejected in his own hometown (Mt 13:58). They heard him preach, "Let the dead bury their own dead" (Lk 9:60), yet saw him weep at the tomb of Lazarus (Jn 11:35). They experienced all of life with him, and he with them, becoming intimate with one another's frailties and strengths. In such an honest, rich environment, true spiritual growth is found.

But to experience all that God had for them, the disciples had to *be there*. Commitment in unity was essential. To leave prematurely, to desert because of some difference of opinion, brought eternal disaster to Judas. We need the whole complement of life together, the good, the bad and the ugly, if we are to know the whole complement of God and his power.

The apostle Paul writes, "I want to know [*ginosko,* know experientially] Christ and the power of his resurrection and the fellowship of sharing in his sufferings, becoming like him in his death, and so, somehow, to attain to the resurrection from the dead" (Phil 3:10).

Unity is fidelity. Jesus promised never to leave his followers (Mt 28:20). He promised that no one could pluck them out of his hand (Jn 10:28). He promised to come back for them (Mt 24:30). He demonstrated his love by laying down his life for them. Jesus Christ modeled fidelity as a healthy and right lifestyle for a member of his Body. He understood that spiritual growth and maturity demand the strength of trust, and trust is earned by faithful commitment.

When the New Testament speaks of Christ's relationship to his church, it often utilizes the imagery of marriage (Jn 3:29; Rev 21:2, 9). Here we see the Bible pointing to the highest form of God-given unity and commitment that a human being can experience as an image for the church. God hates divorce (Mal 2:16) because it betrays radical individualism and a failure to practice love in community.

Transfer growth is often thus in real conflict with the church's mission objective of promoting unity through loving relationships. Transferring, by definition, is all about divorce. John's experience helps us understand.

Marilyn and Don had made their way into the center of their pastor's world. With gifts, invitations and kind words they had befriended John and his entire family. Nothing could have prepared this pastor for the disunity that was created when this couple had a change of heart about their commitment to his ministry.

Their departure, the result of pastoral disenchantment, tore the souls of John and his wife. Worse, disenchantment seemed to spread: suddenly an entire core of people left the church. The exodus permanently cracked the foundations of John's marriage and ministry. His wife, wanting nothing more to do with the church, divorced herself from ministries she once loved. The church struggled to survive as support plummeted.

In a chance encounter with Don and Marilyn in Wal-Mart, John discovered that after three years of separation their leaving still hurt. Trying to be composed, he told me how he experienced that encounter:

> I was overcome with anger and a flood of pain. They were upbeat and told me about the great church they were now actively involved with. My mind wandered as they droned on. I found myself resenting the fact that they had hurt my wife and our church with no apparent concern about the pain they had inflicted on our lives. I couldn't believe their insensitivity as they shared about the wonderful pastor who had so opportunistically profited from the massive exodus we had experienced. I raged inside and vowed to have nothing to do with these insensitive carpetbaggers or their new wonderful church ever again. The only way that I could deal with the pain of that period of my ministry was to mentally annihilate them. I couldn't get through that checkout line fast enough.

Transfer growth is not at all about gathering those who are in the world (Col 1:28) to be saved. It simply gathers the already saved to a new location. Instead of creating an organic cohesion (Eph 1:9-10), it promotes a rending apart of the church through relocation. Christ's prayer regarding oneness (Jn 17) is squandered on those who will not make the investment of commitment and mutual servanthood that Jesus made to his Father and to his church. The body is not built up (Eph 4:12) and the bond of peace is destroyed. Transfer growth promotes division and enables strife to go unreconciled as wounded members of the body simply limp away.

Conclusion

"What then is this bleating of sheep in my ears?" A church that aims to promote the concerns of God should not enable transfer growth. It undermines his sovereignty and cripples spiritual formation. Our deliberate avoidance of this topic has done much more damage than good, for our motivations are centered on self-aggrandizement and not the concerns of the kingdom of God.

This chapter has identified the church as the congregation of believers who gather together locally and form the body of Christ, for the upbuilding of the saints and the promotion of the good news about Jesus Christ. Plurality and unity are God-given components designed to promote spiritual growth and effectively administer the work of the kingdom. It is clear that transfer growth does not foster the fulfillment of these goals. But next let's take an honest look at the perceived benefits that transfer growth brings.

PART 2

3

Have You Any Wool?

Keep watch over yourselves and all the flock of which
the Holy Spirit has made you overseers.
Be shepherds of the church of God,
which he bought with his own blood.

ACTS 20:28

For several decades the church growth movement has capti-
vated the attention of the church around the globe. Fuller Seminary missiologist Donald McGavran and his successors, C. Peter
Wagner, Arthur Glasser, Alan Tippett, Charles Kraft and Paul Hie-
bert, formed a "fraternity of the like-minded" which became "a
potent engine for the dissemination of Church Growth ideas."[1]
Graduates of the school and converts to church growth methods
immediately discovered that the principles applied in ministry created successful environments for growth and evangelization.

The Church Growth Movement
The church growth movement has had a significant impact on the
evangelical church through its philosophies, techniques and strategies for helping churches increase in size, scope and outreach.

"Lyle Schaller, for example, characterizes the emergence of the Church Growth Movement as 'the most influential development of the 1970's on the American religious scene.'"[2]

There are many success stories of churches that became the models of this movement. Jack Hayford's Church on the Way, John Wimber's Vineyard Christian Fellowship, Rick Warren's Saddleback Community Church and Bill Hybels's Willow Creek Community Church are living proof that the principles of church growth work in the United States. Hundreds of pastors have been taught how to do church growth through aggressive programs like the Fuller Institute's seminars and the doctor of ministry program at Fuller Seminary.

"A survey taken in 1991 reported that eighty-six percent of the pastors who read *Leadership* magazine had heard of the church growth movement and that most were positive toward it. Only four percent thought that church growth methods should not be used, whereas eighty-six percent thought that they should be used because these methods were effective."[3] Virtually every evangelical pastor's library contains books on the subject of church growth, and the names of its founders are well known.

Australia has followed America's lead in pursuing church growth principles. Wagner, founding president of the Society for Church Growth, past vice president of the Charles E. Fuller Institute for Evangelism and Church Growth, and author of over thirty books on the subject, has been invited on several occasions to teach in widely acclaimed and well-attended conferences there. The movement's impact in inspiring Australian evangelicals to be reignited in their evangelistic outreach may be captured in Australian Rodger C. Bassham's words: "The most persuasive and extensive evangelical contribution to mission theology has come through the Church Growth Movement."[4]

Paul Yonggi Cho's Yoido Full Gospel Central Church in Seoul has become the world's largest congregation (estimated at 1.2 million in 1999). This feat was accomplished by developing and

applying church growth strategies, in particular small group principles: the church is broken down into structures that allow pastoral
care to effectively meet the needs of the people (see note 7).

Church growth's impact in Cho's life has led him to become an
Asian representative of the movement: "God did not mean for me
to keep this secret for success to myself. In fact, in 1976 he
prompted me to found Church Growth International, so that I
could spread the news and the knowledge of church growth principles to pastors and laymen all over the world . . . I believe that
church growth is going to be one of the major moves of the Holy
Spirit."[5]

Church growth principles and methods are well entrenched in
the life of the evangelical church around the globe. Deeper Christian Life Ministry in Lagos (Nigeria), Vision of the Future Church in
Santa Fe (Argentina) and Jesus Is Lord Fellowship in Manila are all
church growth congregations. Few in Christendom are unaware of
this movement or have not been exposed to the on-site educational experiences, publications and academic offerings created by
church growth advocates.

It was in the 1980s that the church growth movement came of
age. By this time many of its major tenets and programs had been
fully developed and applied in churches throughout the world.
The immediate result appeared to be record-setting church attendance, giving birth to new terms for new sizes of churches.[6]
Church growth, and the exciting science it was developing, was
sweeping the globe.

All this success seemed to indicate that the church growth
movement was on the verge of what McGavran envisioned as the
culmination of the harvest:

The Great Century of Christian Missions may well be followed by a
Greater Century of the Christian Churches. As the churches of Christ
all round the globe, the older churches and the younger churches
banded together, recognize the primacy of discipling those peoples
who have been called of God, and as these churches resolutely

refuse to be turned aside from this harvesting of the ripened grain, there may well result a century of expansion such as has not yet been seen.[7]

This was the powerful vision that spurred on the pioneers of the movement.

No Growth

"Our initial research indicates that there has been *no appreciable growth* in the American evangelical population as a whole over the last ten years." I thought I had misunderstood the church growth professor's statement, but it soon became clear that he was indeed saying the American church had not increased in numbers during the decade of church growth!

The class was Church Growth I at Fuller Seminary's Pasadena campus, March 11, 1991. The professor was one of the leaders in the movement, Peter Wagner. Wagner seemed as surprised and disappointed as we were that the decade of church growth had not increased the size of the Christian population in the land as one would have anticipated.[8] He came to his conclusions while carrying out a growth rate analysis[9] of the 1980s. In his words, "more research needs to be done to determine the ramifications of these findings."

Wagner's surprising conclusions set my mind churning: why had the church not actually grown? Before I pursued the issue I felt it important to verify Wagner's findings, as he had pointed out that they were just preliminary; to suggest major theories or trends based on such initial research would have been premature.

Wagner had used information compiled by the Gallup and Barna research teams. I contacted the Barna Research Group in 1996 at their office in Oxnard, California, and asked its research consultants to dig through their data banks and see if they could find any information that would confirm a growth stagnation trend. The results of their research were sobering, for not only had the church not grown during the 1980s but the stagnation had grown worse in the years since then.

In 1996 the Barna Group reported the results of a further survey:

> The proportion of born again Christians in America has remained unchanged. There has been a modest gain in the number of Catholics, but that gain has been minimized by the slight decline within the Protestant community. In the new 1996 survey, over one-quarter of all Catholics (26%) have beliefs which would classify them as born again Christians, a 63% increase from the proportion of born again Catholics measured in 1991 (16%). The proportion of born again Protestants is currently 57%.[10]

The Barna Group's study also examined the extent to which church attendees were involved in religious activities such as Sunday school, small groups and donating money to a church or fellowship. "Data showed that most measures of religious activity among American adults have remained flat or are experiencing slow decline."[11]

Boomers Too?

The baby boomers had been a popular target of the church growth movement. Since "Baby Boomers are nearly one-third of the total United States population, we recognized that reaching this vast number for Christ represented an unparalleled opportunity given to the Church in this decade of the twentieth century for an evangelism outreach to the unchurched."[12] Courses have been taught, books written, and speakers placed on the circuit with the single message that this was the generation that churches should target.

In light of the Barna reports showing decline in church attendance and people calling themselves born again, I wondered whether the church growth movement had been effective in reaching the boomers. The movement's impact would be shown here.

Statistics from Barna's national 1996 survey summarize the boomers' level of church involvement:

> The 1996 figure for church attendance has declined by one-quarter

from the 1991 level. This is the first time the percentage of attendees has dipped below 40% and the lowest level measured since Barna Research began tracking religious involvement in 1986. . . . Church attendance has dropped most significantly among Baby Boomers—the generation of Americans born between 1946 and 1964.[13]

So even members of this highly sought-after target group failed to show signs of renewal in spite of the church growth movement's best efforts to reach them.

For any growth statistic to remain constant year to year, growth must take place to counteract natural attrition. So it can be assumed that there has been growth within the movement at various points. We also need to consider the possibility that very serious decline might actually have taken place if the church growth movement had not implemented its many new concepts. More drastic reductions in church involvement and attendance may have actually been staved off by such efforts.

Still, we must address the hard facts and consider where these findings take us. The church growth movement was founded with the hope of increasing God's kingdom, yet current research shows that numerical success has eluded us. What has happened to cause these surprising results?

The Grand Illusion

The answer lies in the definition of the term *illusion*. The *American Heritage Dictionary* defines an illusion as "an erroneous perception of reality." It had been widely believed that the church growth movement had brought significant increases in the population of the church through conversion growth.[14] There can be no question that all of us involved in church growth assumed that we were reaching more and more people for Christ and increasing the numbers of those who were being saved. Now we discover that in fact a very different trend has been established. How could we have been so ignorant of these facts? The error is in the difference between what we *preach* and what we *practice*.

We preach reaching the lost. No movement in the history of the church has spent more money or time on researching and developing evangelistic programs than the church growth movement. In programs like D. James Kennedy's Evangelism Explosion[15] seminars, designed to knock at the doors of the unchurched, and the many small group and evangelistic Bible study materials available, leading people to Christ has been the assumed single most important task. This orientation has created a sense of well-being in the movement as growing churches gave the impression of dynamically reaching the lost for the Lord Jesus Christ.

There can be no doubt that several churches do grow this way and are making utterly sincere efforts to fulfill the Great Commission. Saddleback Valley Community Church of Mission Viejo, California, for instance, has created a composite unchurched personage, Saddleback Sam, to help the church's leaders focus programs on meeting the needs of the unchurched. Saddleback Sam influences everything from parking to carpet colors, childcare to worship themes. Great sensitivity is expended to capture a chance to introduce unchurched people to Christ.[16]

Another stellar example of evangelistic integrity is the Willow Creek Community Church in Barrington, Illinois. This church forged its ministry from the ground up with reference to the needs of the unchurched.[17] Pastor Bill Hybels and his colleagues knocked on the doors of their community with surveys to try to discover what the church lacked in the eyes of the secular world. With the resulting information in hand, Hybels and his team what developed a seventeen-thousand-person worship center whose success is a direct reflection of their efforts to honor Christ by seeking the lost. A mall-like atmosphere, full-scale gym facilities, messages in drama, and massive ministry packages are all geared toward "seekers" as Willow Creek Community Church tries to reach the unchurched neighbors next door.

These churches reflect the best of the church growth movement's efforts to carry out our Lord's directives in seeking the lost.

Bringing in the harvest was our Lord's passion, and his words have been the single unifying theme of the many diverse entities under the church growth umbrella. " 'My food,' said Jesus, 'is to do the will of him who sent me and to finish his work. Do you not say, "Four months more and then the harvest?" I tell you, open your eyes and look at the fields! They are ripe for harvest'" (Jn 4:34-35). It has been naturally assumed that churches involved in the movement were focused on this central charge of reaching the lost.

But if the church growth movement has been so seeker sensitive, why are church attendance and conversions declining in the Protestant church?

Sadly, we have shifted our priorities and purpose. We have been living in illusion: we think we are about the Lord's work and we preach reaching the lost, but in fact we are primarily attracting already-churched people.

The Already Churched

If this is the case, we should expect to see the stagnant growth curve we are currently experiencing. Sheep stealing allows some churches to grow while others decline, creating the illusion of growth without affecting the kingdom count. Is this the missing link to the startling riddle Wagner discovered?

Jesus' disciples struggled with the spiritual, intangible nature of the kingdom of God. In their eyes Rome had a *real* kingdom, with buildings, armies, commerce, subjects, power. The unsubstantiated spiritual kingdom of which Jesus spoke was a concept difficult for them to grasp.

Nonetheless Jesus was unwavering in devotion to this spiritual kingdom. He never sought popularity or personal gain, in spite of Satan's temptations and the crowds' desires and accolades. Jesus was focused on souls. This was the work his Father had commissioned. Each person who discovered God's salvation plan was another subject freed from hell's grasp and added to the Lord's kingdom. These are the numbers God is interested in; this is the *kingdom count*.

Conversions constitute a significant part of the work of God: "For the Son of Man came to seek and to save what was lost" (Lk. 19:10). When the last of the elect is harvested, the current age will come to an end.[18] Christ's parousia will frame the climactic finish of the church's work on earth, as God gathers his fought-for and saved children.[19] The kingdom count needs to be a primary goal for us as it was for Jesus. Adding to the kingdom count should be church growth's finest contribution to the cause of Christ.

But apparently there can be church growth that has nothing to do with the kingdom count. If a church grew simply through transfer growth, there would be no increase in the evangelical community, in spite of the appearance of greater things being accomplished. Transfer growth by its very nature can occur only if there is transfer decline somewhere else—bringing no numerical gain for the kingdom.

Wagner offers an illustration that addresses the issue of kingdom growth[20] versus transfer growth:

> Some church growth is Kingdom growth and some isn't. Suppose that First Methodist church for example grows from five hundred members to one thousand members in ten years. Statistically that is good church growth. But suppose further analysis shows that a nearby Methodist church of one hundred fifty members closed its doors and one hundred of them joined First Methodist. Then a Church of the Nazarene split and two hundred of its members came in. Another one hundred moved into town and brought letters of transfer with them. The final one hundred were men and women who had no previous church affiliation and who were led to Christ through the witness of the members of First Methodist. How much of the growth was Kingdom growth? Obviously only the one hundred who were converted from the world, or twenty percent! Eighty percent was nothing more than what one author has called "the circulation of the saints."[21]

So transfer growth can cause a particular church to prosper yet produce a net result that adds little to the kingdom of God.

Suspicions Confirmed?

Critics of the church growth movement have for years alleged that the touted growth has not come from conversions. Traditional churches' resentment toward the movement has often been fueled by the luring away of their parishioners to more dynamic church growth settings. One critic has remarked that church growth is "nothing more than the rearranging of the ecclesiastical furniture."

I long dismissed such criticisms as envious, resentful comments from those who do not like change. In hindsight, perhaps some of their observations were more accurate than I imagined. If the practice of aggressive transfer growth has actually been widespread, several questions begin to gain a new focus.

Could this explain the lack of overall growth in the evangelical population in spite of the best efforts of the church growth movement? Has transfer growth become the central means of expansion for megachurches and metachurches? If transfers play as large a role as preliminary research indicates, what are the implications for the universal body of Christ and the church growth movement? These questions and more demand our attention.

Denial is often the first reaction to shocking news. For a time I simply could not grasp the concept that the efforts of the church growth movement may have consisted predominantly of stealing sheep from sister churches. That was not my motivation for becoming a church growth pastor, and I knew that the founders of the movement sincerely desired to reach lost souls and increase the kingdom count. I needed more information, so I began digging deeper to find out: how common is sheep stealing—really?

American Church Growth

Perhaps the flagship church of the evangelical movement during the late 1980s and early 1990s was the Evangelical Free Church of Fullerton, California. Over five thousand people made their way to the worship service on its impressive campus each Sunday. Thousands more attended sessions in its massive Sunday school structure. Under the preaching and teaching of Pastor Chuck Swindoll, this church had become a church growth success story, focusing on relational and service aspects of Christian ministry.

In 1991 I was on this church's campus studying the dynamics of their ministry as part of my postgraduate work at Fuller Seminary. My research included an on-the-spot survey of worshipers as they entered the church building on Sunday morning. The questionnaire was designed to explore what had motivated people to select this church as a church home. For example, it asked how they were first attracted to the church, how long they had attended, and whether they had had previous membership in another church. An astonishing 90-plus percent of those interviewed indicated that they had transferred to the Evangelical Free Church of Fullerton from another church![22]

Later in a private interview with Swindoll, I asked if he could guess how many people were in his church as a result of transferring from another congregation. He said, "I would guess 80 to 85 percent of our people are from other churches."

I was surprised both at the survey's results and at the pastor's accurate understanding of this phenomenon. I had seen the Evangelical Free Church as one of America's best church growth settings. It had a powerful Sunday school program, solid evangelical teaching, and a pastor whose gifted preaching style is second to none. Yet transfer growth, not conversion growth, was clearly the major source of the church's increase in size and membership.

The Lake Avenue Congregational Church in Pasadena, California was another interesting case study. Paul Cedar had been seeing tremendous growth during his pastorate there; in fact Lake Avenue was the home church of many of the principal leaders in the church growth movement. During a discussion with Carl George of the Fuller Institute on Church Growth, I asked, "What was the major contributing factor to Lake Avenue's growth?"

He replied, "Lake Avenue Congregational Church has collected the remains of fifteen to twenty churches over the years. This has been a major factor in its growth."

Ted Haggard is the founder and pastor of the New Life Church in Colorado Springs, Colorado. The church's phenomenal growth and membership of over five thousand people have been written about in the *New York Times* and the *Washington Post* and won attention on ABC and BBC news programs. Jack Hayford, of the Church on the Way, states, "In my perspective, Ted Haggard is one of today's top ten rising spiritual leaders: a key man."[23] Haggard is committed to conversion growth.

In *Primary Purpose: Making It Hard for People to Go to Hell from Your City*, Haggard reiterates Wagner's warning regarding the treadmill effect of transfer growth. "The illusion of the past says, 'If my church is growing, then it is making a difference in our city.' The reality is that if one life-giving church grows because another is declining, then there is no net difference in the social and cultural makeup of the city."[24] His book, by design and title, is intent on refocusing the church on its primary purpose of reaching the lost.

Yet even Haggard's impressive ministry acknowledges that over 50 percent of its Sunday morning worshipers have come from other churches. "On an average Sunday morning, the congregation at New Life Church is made up of about fifty percent transfers from other churches and about fifty percent people who were either born-again or have recommitted their lives to Christ in our church."[25] Clearly transfer growth constitutes a very large share of the church growth phenomenon even where a deliberate attempt is made to focus on conversion growth.

Around the Globe

The church growth movement and its philosophies have been welcomed beyond United States boundaries, by European, Asian, Latin American and African churches. As noted earlier, perhaps the most voracious appetite for church growth materials can be found in Australia. Here evangelical churches sought and applied church growth techniques for most of the 1990s. Church growth seminars and conferences were frequent, featuring many of America's foremost experts in the field. Many of Australia's churches have grown, but what kind of growth did they experience—conversion growth or transfer growth?

John Waterhouse, editor at Albatross Books in Sutherland, Australia, drew my attention to an Australian publication that surveyed over thirty denominations in an effort to record the experiences of the church in a changing Australia. *The Winds of Change* is an exhaustive landmark document produced by the National Church Life Survey Committee; it was developed and resourced through the Uniting Church Board Mission and the Anglican Diocese of Sydney's Home Mission Society. Anglicans, Baptists, the Church of the Nazarene, Lutherans, Presbyterians, the Salvation Army, Foursquare Gospel and Wesleyans were but a few of the groups included in the survey. It covered a wide spectrum of topics pertaining to the life of the church in Australia, including the decline and growth of its churches.

Five categories were developed. "Visitors" are people claiming to be visiting the congregation in which they completed the survey forms. "Newcomers to congregational life" have attended their present congregation for under five years and previously were not regularly attending anywhere else. "Denominational switchers" have attended their present congregation for under five years and previously were attending a congregation of a different denomination. "Transfers within a denomination" have attended a congregation of the same denomination. "Longer term attenders" have attended their present congregation for more than five years.[26] These groups were created to help identify the patterns of growth within Australia's denominations and churches.

The study came up with some sobering results. *The Winds of Change* identified "twenty-eight percent of attenders in the study group as having changed congregations in the past five years."[27] Although this figure seems modest compared to American trends, bear in mind that Australia is holding on to old denominational value systems that once existed in the United States. These old values emphasized loyalty to the church and denomination in which one was were brought up. One should never leave it for any reason. Thus 28 percent is a staggeringly high figure for the transferring of Australians out of their home churches. This points to a shift in values, an "apparent decline in loyalty amongst church attenders."[28]

In some denominations the level of transfer was as high as 43 percent,[29] indicating a drastic turnover in just a five-year span. Australians no longer accept their lot with the church of their birth; they are becoming more discriminating in their taste for church performance, and churches appear to be supporting the membership transferring trends.

The study attributes denominational growth in Australia largely to transfer growth: "Much of the growth in these denominations is fueled by switching rather than by a wide intake of people previously not involved with a congregation. In Pentecostal denominations, switchers outnumber newcomers to church life by almost three to one."[30] "These results underline the fact that denominational switching [transfer growth] is one of the important forces affecting the denominational balances in this country. Denominations with high levels of switchers are among the fastest growing. Switching is a key aspect of their growth."[31]

Transfer growth is also the main source of growth for Australia's larger churches. "In congregations of more than five hundred people, twenty-four percent of attenders are switchers and thirteen percent are transfers" (37 percent transfer growth). In the fastest-growing church settings transfer growth plays a key role: "Congregations which have grown by fifty percent in the past five years are likely to contain twice the percentage of switchers [of] stable or declining congregations."[32]

The authors observe that growth of the Australian church may not involve the abundant conversions that were originally envisioned. They summarize: "Writing in the American context, [Canadian Reginald] Bibby has suggested that church growth is mainly the result of a circulation of the saints rather than the results of evangelism in the community (Bibby, 1978). The [National Church Life Survey] lends qualified support to this idea."[33]

As a young pastor serving in New England, I tasted the fruit of transfer growth. It appears that once you institute programming that inspires church renewal, the ministry becomes a magnet. Transfers are often the lifeblood of a revival, renewal or church plant. Transferees can offer experienced gifts of teaching and discipling to newer converts. Their enthusiasm can foster a sense of prestige, stroking emotional needs of the pastor and the congregation: these people have chosen *your* church as the most dynamic work in the area.

Transfer growth is tempting because of the many assets it brings to the receptor church. But I fear the evangelical arm of the church has become addicted to this form of growth at the expense of engaging in the true work of the gospel. If so, how did this happen?

Conclusion

This chapter reviewed the development of the church growth movement and the strong interest its philosophies have generated in the church worldwide. But there is a cause for concern: the lack of a rise in the evangelical population in the church. It appears that transfer growth is the actual source of much of the church growth movement's success, both in the United States and around the globe.

"Keep watch over yourselves," Paul solemnly warned the Ephesian elders regarding their care of God's flock. This is our charge as well, and it includes rightly discerning the impact our programs and philosophies have on the broader kingdom of God. Transfer growth is affecting the church, and it is the church's responsibility to examine it carefully and honestly.

4

Counting Sheep

*Satan rose up against Israel and incited David to take a census
of Israel. So David said to Joab, . . . "Go and count the Israelites
from Beersheba to Dan. Then report back to me so that
I may know how many there are."
    But Joab replied, . . . "Why does my lord want to do this?"*
                                            1 CHRONICLES 21:1-3

Human beings have always measured success in numbers. Scriptural examples include the exacting count of 153 fish caught by the disciples after Jesus' resurrection (Jn 21:11) and the size of the crowd that converted to Christianity after Peter's compelling sermon (Acts 2:41). Our newscasts greedily cover the daily rises and slumps of the stock market. Numbers provide fast and objective data that clearly indicate growth or decline. They are a natural means by which ministries and churches can measure the success of their evangelistic strategies.

The use of numbers, specifically census taking, is not immediately associated with sin in the Bible. The book of Numbers, beginning with its very first chapter and verse, is perhaps the most obvious example of the use of statistics as a legitimate means of confirming the hand of God in blessing his people.

Some data collection actually has pragmatic and cultic significance in the divine economy. For example, God instructs Moses to take a census so that the Lord can be paid a ransom offering for each fighting man's life (Ex 30:12).

Double-Edged Sword

But numbers are a double-edged sword. There is a power in the amassing of them that kindles our fascination with success. This path leads to a host of sins: we may easily leave the realm of trusting God and slip into self-aggrandizement.

This was Joab's fear when King David ordered a census of his fighting men (1 Chron 21:3). Was David testing God's provision?[1] Or worse, was he claiming to be a great king because of the number of his subjects? We do not know David's true motives, but we do know God's displeasure with this census: "So the LORD sent a plague on Israel, and seventy thousand men of Israel fell dead" (1 Chron 21:14).

The love of anything, including numbers, could be called the "root of all kinds of evil." If your affection and obsession usurps the greatest commandment, "Love the Lord your God with all your heart and with all your soul and with all your mind" (Mt 22:37), then you have made what you love a demigod.[2] Counting the increase of your ministry or church can weave a very powerful emotional attachment that leads some away from the heart of God.

Concerned Responses

Since the early 1960s, skepticism about the integrity of Donald McGavran's church growth theories and use of statistics has been present in many branches of Christendom. Several researchers issued warnings about the new church growth movement's heavy reliance on numerical data.

"The renewed interest in Church Growth and the stimulating studies of Donald McGavran are important," wrote Hans-Reudi Weber of the Ecumenical Institute. ". . . However they often use man's and not God's arithmetic as the measure of growth".[3] C. René Padilla, writing in Latin America, where the charismatic movement and the church growth movement have converged to create a powerful spirit of revival, warns that the church must be cautious about the dangers of: "the philosophy of statistical success."[4] Biblical scholar Ralph P. Martin also sounded a note of caution:

> One final slogan that contains a lot of unexamined and questionable assumptions is church growth. Its philosophy undergirds a great deal of thinking and planning to do with the church's mission in the world in the 1970's. . . . But let's be clear that witness and numerical growth are not the same. . . . It is God's church that we are talking about, and He alone can produce the growth. "I will build my church" (Matthew 16:18) runs counter to a lot of popular sentiment current today, expressed by those who imagine that they can bring in the kingdom of God with a slide-rule and a set of log tables.[5]

Hear No Evil

These early warnings were easy to ignore. First, McGavran's motives for using numbers were to create a system that would hold mission stations accountable for their "kingdom productivity" (conversions). Up to this point many organizations around the globe were claiming to be involved in the advancement of the gospel yet were actually doing little to lead the lost to Christ. McGavran sought to change that. Through the keeping and analysis of empirical data, the value of each ministry's evangelistic contribution could be objectively surveyed.

Not surprisingly, established missions that were receiving denominational support and money[6] but had virtually no accountability were quickly defensive about this new approach. Many negative comments about the use of church growth statistics stemmed from a fear of being weighed in the scales and found wanting. Such objections were assumed to be the cries of those who were about to lose their programs. It was easy to doubt the sincerity of their concern over the use of numbers.

Second, during the time of McGavran's research many mainline churches and denominations were suffering. In *Understanding Church Growth and Decline, 1950-1978,* Dean Hoge and David Roozen state that there were "shocking rates of decline in the traditional church."[7] At the same time the new church growth ministries appeared to be growing. Cries of foul play seemed motivated by jealousy and fear. There was an underlying perception that failing institutions hardly had the credibility to give advice to the burgeoning church growth movement.

The point needs to be made that the church growth movement has used numbers effectively to chart the life patterns of churches, thereby developing analysis that objectively identifies growth and decline patterns.[8] This has given Christendom an accurate tool to use in measuring a ministry's growth and performance.

Without numbers, gross subjectivity simply buries any valid analysis of most ministries. With numbers and statistics, diseased and dying ministries can be identified and health can potentially be restored. This contribution of the church growth movement has had a tremendous positive impact on the church universally.

Love of Numbers

Regrettably, in spite of the positive contributions of the movement, Joab's concern about how the love of numbers can usurp God's place points to a weakness at the heart of the church growth movement. Like medicine that is prescribed to heal but that by virtue of the well-being it produces becomes addictive, numbers can become the obsession of a ministry. The result is a transition from kingdom growth and kingdom concern to personal ministry growth and personal ministry concerns.

Padilla warned of this pending shift of the primary focus of the church when he cautioned Latin American churches against an "excessive emphasis on numbers." Such an obsession would be a new god, leading to the new religion of "numerolatry."[9]

Transfer growth embraces modernity on the plains of numerical success. By using numbers in the same fashion that the capitalistic culture of business uses them, the church growth movement has ultimately given numbers the authority to define success or failure in a ministry. The use of numbers in this fashion is a standard and chartered principle of the church growth movement.[10]

"The two most easily recognizable hallmarks of secularization in America are the exaltation of numbers and of technique. Both are prominent in the megachurch movement at a popular level. In its fascination with statistics and data . . . this movement is characteristically modern,"[11] says culture critic Os Guinness.

In a commentary on 1 Corinthians, Gordon Fee warns about the dangers of using human hands to build God's kingdom:

It is unfortunately possible for people to attempt to build the church out of every imaginable human system predicated on merely worldly wisdom, be it philosophy, "pop" psychology, managerial techniques, relational "good feelings," or what have you. But at the final judgment, all such building (and perhaps countless other forms, where systems have become more important than the gospel itself) will be shown for what it is: something merely human, with no character of Christ or his gospel in it. Often, of course, the test may come this side of the final one, and in such an hour of stress that which has been built of modern forms of Sophia usually comes tumbling down.[12]

Many church growth pastors have in fact struggled with David's sin as anxiety about numbers creeps into their ministries. Jack Hayford muses:

I confess to sporadic bouts of doubt and cynicism. These intrusions of carnality into my pastor-heart spring from the temptation to play the church numbers game, creating my pastoral self-image based on attendance figures. Let me say that I do believe in counting sheep. . . . However, the Word also warns against becoming more concerned with numerical strength than with God's ways. . . . The challenge for me is to listen to the Holy Spirit and to quit measuring my pastoral success by playing the numbers game.[13]

The telltale warning sign of the transition from the use of numbers as a tool to exalting numbers as a god is the compromising of our motivations and biblical integrity. "If you love me," says Jesus, "you will obey what I command" (Jn 14:15). Becoming obsessed with growth can cause us to bend biblical standards. At this point we begin "dining with the devil." We end up loving to count the sheep in the fold more than loving to obey the shepherd.

The Work of the Church

Historically, conversions to the Lord Jesus Christ were always the primary focus of the apostles and the church's work.[14] The same was true of the church growth movement at its inception. For example, C. Peter Wagner stated, "The major burden of the Church Growth Movement has been to assist new conversion growth, the kind of church growth that most parallels true kingdom growth."[15]

According to Charles Van Engen, yearning for numerical growth is an essential mark of the true church:

> Yearning for numerical growth originates in a number of important motifs found in Scripture, all of which point to the same essential reality. The *universal intention* of God in the Old Testament, the *gathering* in the New Testament, the *finding* of the lost sheep, the *building* toward fullness, and the picture of *growth* all point to something in the Church's nature which makes it yearn to incorporate more and more people within itself. There are likewise many biblical images of the Church that suggest this earnest desire. Whether the Church is viewed as the people of God, the new Israel, the sheepfold, the planting, the building, or the body, there is always a driving energy within it. This is the growth principle by which the Church has always expressed her nature in "yearning" to incorporate more and more men and women within the bounds of God's grace. It is a movement, a spirit, a presence which has pushed the Church from Pentecost to the present in an ever-widening, ever-outward, ever-enlarging sphere of life and influence in the world.[16]

Tragically, broad evangelical participation in transfer growth indicates that another goal in the church growth movement has rapidly overcome this original objective of reaching the lost. The movement has shifted its focus. No longer are we seeking lost, unsaved people, nor are we laboring in the harvest; instead we are raiding one another's churches.

What has caused this trend to develop? I am sure that one contributing factor is the emphasis on numerical growth. The emphasis on numbers has inspired lax standards in analysis of the source of our growth.

Cheap Growth

Cheap growth—growth that steals and avoids the labor of evangelization and discipleship—is fast and efficient; it graphs well in a church's year-end report. From a purely objective perspective it is highly profitable. This deceptive form of growth (if we can call it growth) may well be the god of "numerolatry" that Padilla warned us about so many years ago.

How could cheap growth generated by transfers become a mainstay, especially when the entire church growth movement had seemed so committed to what Wagner called "church growth eyes"[17]—eyes that focus the efforts of the church on the goal of conversion growth? As we analyze the work of the movement's founder, McGavran, we will begin to see the seeds of concepts that would give birth to the practice of transfer growth.

Sheep stealing by its nature is insidious. It is like a virus, attaching itself to healthy cells. McGavran's work involved solid and productive research, and his fresh ideas were groundbreaking. Yet hidden in the recesses of his work were three principles that would lead to justification of transfer growth. In the years following McGavran's seminal publications, these three principles would be absorbed into the mainstream philosophies of the church growth movement. Transfer growth would be accepted with them, becoming popularized through publications and taught through the seminars and courses that hawked church growth wares.

The three are the "Maximization Principle," the "Transferring of Resources Principle" and the "Numerical Principle." Examining the evolution of these principles will allow us to see how transfer growth developed with them.

Bridges of God

During the mid-1950s McGavran developed missions strategies that would forever change the way we do ministry. Drawing on his work with churches and mission boards in India, McGavran authored a landmark book called *The Bridges of God*. In it he outlined his concern about the apparent shift in primary objectives of the mission stations in India. He describes a dangerous and unproductive pattern that was emerging. Missionaries were frustrated with the poor conversion rate of the Hindus. "Small [conversion] response was *not* expected by the early missionaries."[18] When conversions were few, "a vicious circle was established: the few becoming Christian one by one set such a [slow] pattern [for growth] that it was difficult for a Christward movement to be started."[19] Discouragement fueled by lack of response to the gospel led the India mission stations into a diversion toward "secondary aims." "When it became apparent that the people of the land were not espousing Christianity in any but the smallest numbers, the institutional work appeared as more solid, more tangible, more rewarding."[20] So evangelizing the heathen gave way to social programming. "Sometimes the mission was pressed into educational work. . . . Sometimes the diversion to secondary aims came through medicine. Orphanages, schools, hospitals, or agricultural enterprises were developed."[21]

"Generations of missionaries," notes McGavran, "devoted their entire lives to social agendas. They found their consolation and satisfaction in the service of the non-Christian nation, through the general alleviation of ignorance and suffering, and the creation of a friendly attitude toward the mission."[22] So complete was this shift away from the original charter of winning the lost to Christ that "not only did missions turn to secondary aims but they came to consider them primary."[23]

From McGavran's perspective, the mission leaders' acceptance of their new, secular role compounded the decline in evangelistic efforts. "Were such Christian leaders to be asked to evaluate their tasks in terms of the Christianization of peoples, they would quite likely reply that they were not interested in an increase of mere numbers, or that what they were doing (through social programming) was Christianization of the finest sort."[24]

Beyond the local missionaries' blindness, McGavran points to the sending boards and churches' head-in-the-sand philosophy regarding success in missions. "The sending boards and churches made no distinction between mission enterprises serving the primary aim (evangelization) and those serving these secondary aims. All were equally valuable mission works. Indeed, the need of promotion among the sending churches turned all into grand works."[25] Kenneth Grubb describes this new missionary enterprise as "the hum of mighty workings [that] has fascinated us, as the flame fascinates the moth."[26] McGavran concludes, "The discipling of peoples was a matter to . . . which neither the missionary nor the mission, nor the home boards, nor the churches paid much attention. This is scarcely the atmosphere in which Christward movements of peoples can originate. . . . Such a typical institutionalized Mission Station Approach actually prevents the start of Christward movements."[27]

The flat line of no growth was the catalyst as McGavran began searching for a new way to evaluate and stimulate mission stations in India. This was not an obvious or easy task:

> Evangelization, the central task, is beset with difficulties. Congregations and denominations become static. Most Christians never win anyone to the Christian faith. Some non-Christian populations are resistant. They must hear the Gospel, yet so must those who are responsive. How can we most effectively communicate the Gospel and multiply sound churches? What are the best methods? When is

non-growth the result of weak faith and when of poor methods? . . .
We need light.[28]

That light came as McGavran worked to develop accountability
structures through data analysis.[29] Statistical methods were honed
to determine the growth rates of mission stations and thus their
importance to the kingdom. "The Numerical approach is essential
to understanding church growth. The church is made up of count-
able people and there is nothing particularly spiritual in not counting them. . . . Without it, effective administration and accurate
forecast would be impossible."[30]

With empirical data, McGavran was confident that an accurate
picture of world evangelization would emerge as growth factors—
type of mission, size of staff, number of churches in the mission,
annual cost of the mission, cost per person for each convert in the
mission, and rate of growth—were recorded. These statistics, when
translated into a numerical assessment, would identify for a missions board the ministry's fastest-growing and least productive
areas.

The Maximization Principle

McGavran's "Maximization Principle" points to a survival of the fittest program that would ultimately eliminate nonproductive ministries. *The Bridges of God* articulates the principle clearly. "The
thesis of this book may now be fully stated. The era has come
when Christian Missions should hold lightly all mission station
work which cannot be proved to nurture growing churches, and
should support the Christ-ward movements within Peoples as long
as they continue to grow at the rate of 50 per cent per decade or
more. This is to-day's strategy."[31] In this fashion, McGavran could
envision the creation of a competitive, aggressive, crack team of
churches and mission stations, earnestly invested in generating
conversion numbers in the harvest.

With this bold new Maximization Principle in missions, McGavran threatened to bring to an end the age of the "good ol' boys"

club. The support of stagnant ministries that did not produce conversions suddenly fell into grave jeopardy. McGavran's proposal would use growth and productivity as the yardstick, potentially eliminating all dead wood.[32]

Soon theology emerged that was designed to establish the biblical integrity of the Maximization Principle. Wagner's Church Growth I class provides examples in the sessions on "Biblical Principles": "Accountability is knowing the Master's will and doing it." Wagner told students, "Stewardship (a) understands the mysteries of God, and (b) knows that to be faithful is to be successful."[33]

Good stewardship became the high goal of the church growth movement, based on the Maximization Principle. It was a foundation block in the building of a philosophy of ministry and was seen as the starting point for the work of the gospel. Wagner called attention to the apostle Paul's words: "Let a man so consider us, as servants of Christ and stewards of the mysteries of God. Moreover it is required in stewards that one be found faithful" (1 Cor 4:1-2 NKJV).[34]

The movement defined stewardship as productivity, with reference to the parable of the talents:

> The man who had received the five talents brought the other five. "Master," he said, "you entrusted me with five talents. See, I have gained five more."
>
> His master replied, "Well done, good and faithful servant! You have been faithful with a few things, I will put you in charge of many things. Come and share your master's happiness!" (Mt 25:20-21)

Churches that were not being productive—showing numerical increase—were, by deduction, not being faithful stewards. Growth reveals a church or ministry's proper response to the Lord. Every ministry logically should feel an obligation to grow, for we are entrusted with the sacred responsibility of sharing the mystery of salvation. "Anyone who knows Jesus Christ as his Lord and Saviour must *desire ardently* that others should share that knowledge and must rejoice when the number of those who do is multiplied. Where this desire and this rejoicing are absent, we must ask whether something is not wrong at the very center of the church's life."[35]

This evangelistic zeal compelled the church growth movement to not only fix but if need be eliminate ministries that were not growing. Wagner argued, "Why continue to nurse a non-fruit-bearing plant? Cut it down!" He pointed to Luke 13:6-9:

> Then he told this parable: "A man had a fig tree, planted in his vineyard, and he went to look for fruit on it, but did not find any. So he said to the man who took care of the vineyard, 'For three years now I've been coming to look for fruit on this fig tree and haven't found any. Cut it down! Why should it use up the soil?"
>
> " 'Sir,' the man replied, 'leave it alone for one more year, and I'll dig around it and fertilize it. If it bears fruit next year, fine! If not, then cut it down.'"

The Abusive Underside

As positive as the Maximization Principle appears, "pruning," its abusive underside, brought open season on any church or ministry that was not showing numerical evidence of converts to the faith. The principle quickly evolved in a philosophy of ministry that justified growing churches' tendencies to steal sheep from other churches. "Holding them lightly" (McGavran) was interpreted to justify considering other churches not colaborers but often part of the mission field! Watching them die was part of natural selection, as the church pressed on toward the survival of the fittest.

Thus although the Maximization Principle was originally intended to help the church become more effective, it led to many abuses. In time, stagnant or declining Christian ministries were brutalized. They were, after all, not only expendable but actually drains on kingdom resources.

This was a topic frequently discussed in Wagner's Church Growth classes at Fuller. The mercy killing of a stagnant church was a classic application of the Maximization Principle. In class discussions, students often expressed approval of killing off declining ministries.

But the Maximization Principle misses the reality that evangelization and the growth of a ministry were never intended to be competitive. The gospel is not some sort of a divine race.

Believers undergo a pilgrimage of development referred to as the sanctification process—becoming more like Christ through the pursuit of holiness. That process may mean that it is inappropriate to take advantage of a church that is struggling or at some other point of growth. Perhaps God is taking the body of believers through a phase of Christian maturing that requires some stressful pressure to expose and eradicate sin. Interference with that process may well be interference with the hand of God.

In 1987 the little church I was pastoring suffered an agonizing split. In its wake I invested time in trying to heal wounds and reestablish relationship with the people who had left. This was undoubtedly the single most important growth period of my pastoral development. During this time I was confronted by my nature, the nature of all human beings and the grace of God, particularly the depth of his love. The depths of my theology and Christian character were forged on the anvil of this experience.

Many of the people from whom I had become estranged had been for the past several weeks attending another church. The pastor of this church was a brother with whom I had spent several hours in various ministry-related events. I invited him over to talk about the importance of repentance, forgiveness and reconciliation. Acknowledging that these are the very essence of the gospel of Jesus Christ, I explained that now was a "learning moment" for me and the estranged people to find healing in the work of the cross. I needed my fellow pastor's support and understanding so that I could pastor in this difficult situation. Specifically, I asked him not to support transfer growth from our church to his, but instead turn people back to enter a healing process.

His response stunned me. "When they walked through the door of my church, they became my sheep," he replied. "Whoever steps through that door, I become their pastor."

I briefly protested that such a position would cause great damage to our church. He simply smiled, got up and walked out of my life. His view of the situation, I assume, was that my ministry was not producing fruit at the moment and needed to be pruned; his ministry was the people's salvation.[36]

This experience points to the unfortunate cost of the Maximization Principle—people. When church leaders are wrapped up in the smallness of their worlds, it is often difficult to remain objective and sensitive to discern how the Lord is working.

The Transferring of Resources Principle

A second McGavran principle that fosters transfer growth was the "Transferring of Resources Principle." Here numbers do more than identify successful ministries and offer support to their growth (the Maximization Principle). Numbers also define what unproductive ministries should die so as to free up their resources to more fruitful endeavors. In his early writings McGavran developed the concept:

> During the decade just passed the "Mission Station Approach" churches experienced a 20 per cent growth in membership. This means they grew chiefly by excess of births over deaths. During the same decade the growing "People Movement" churches had a 60 per cent growth in membership. . . . What would our proposed strategy mean if applied in such a situation? . . . Leave 30 per cent of the budget with the Mission Station Approach mission and move 70 per cent of the resources to the growing People Movement mission. . . . If winning men for Christ and the establishment of churches is the goal of missions, then such transfers need to be considered most seriously by leaders of the Christian work.[37]

McGavran's main interest was to show how much more productive homogenous unit evangelism was over the standard Mission Station Approach, and that support for the more successful ministry justifies the rechanneling of resources toward its ministry. Here the original concept of transferring resources is applied in theory. The church growth movement would develop this concept into the transferring of finances and shifting church populations based on a church's vitality and people's satisfaction levels.[38] In this fashion, through "church growth eyes" the disembodiment of a church was not necessarily a bad thing—especially if other more productive ministries prospered.

Although the concept seems harsh, the church growth movement could point to Scriptures supporting both the Lord's seriousness in seeing his work carried out and the concept of transferring resources. Wagner's Church Growth I lectures cited these verses:

> Then the man who had received the one talent came. "Master," he said, "I knew that you are a hard man, harvesting where you have not sown and gathering where you have not scattered seed. So I was afraid and went out and hid your talent in the ground. See, here is what belongs to you."
>
> His master replied, "You wicked, lazy servant! So you knew that I harvest where I have not sown and gather where I have not scattered seed? Well then, you should have put my money on deposit with the bankers, so that when I returned I would have received it back with interest.
>
> "Take the talent from him and give it to the one who has the ten talents. For everyone who has will be given more, and he will have an abundance. Whoever does not have, even what he has will be taken from him. And throw that worthless servant outside, into the darkness, where there will be weeping and gnashing of teeth." (Mt 25:24-30)[39]

Could the Transferring of Resources Principle ever be legitimately applied in church settings? In 1988 I was involved in the closing of a "dead" inner-city church. We had consulted with the few remaining members of the congregation and had convinced them to sell the property and turn the assets over to the denomination. With those funds we hired a new pastor, rented an auditorium and began a new church plant in the city. This church prospered and today has a vital ministry. I think this exemplifies the kind of productive reallocation of resources that McGavran had in mind.

Church growth pastors sometimes see transfer growth as a parallel "transferring of resources." When growth occurs from transferring memberships, the "fat sheep don't wander" ideology rings in their ears. People are selecting the better (Maximization Principle) and transferring their assets (Transferring of Resources Principle); what is wrong with that? In fact Carl George dubs smaller churches that lose members to larger churches "feeder churches."[40] Given this level of justification, sheep stealing prospers.

McGavran's "Transferring of Resources principle" calls for a judgment call, a death certificate if you will, to be pronounced on a church or ministry. In the Matthew 25:24-30 passage the Lord is the implied judge. But in church growth settings, often the prospering church or the disgruntled sheep are the judges. Can either of these parties honestly speak for God? Do they truly know what processes are under way or what lessons God is attempting to teach?

Several years ago a friend told me how his grandfather had the dubious task of moving a cemetery. One of the caskets dug up from the 1800s accidentally broke open. Inside the cover of the casket there were well-defined scratch marks. The woman's body was twisted and contorted, and one foot had actually punched through the bottom of the casket. This person had accidentally been buried alive.

To dispose of people and resources from a church not yet dead is to open ourselves up to causing long-lasting harm.

The Numerical Growth Principle

Throughout McGavran's work, the primary standard for identifying growth was numerical increase. It was an objective, simple way to assess the "fruits" of any given church or mission station. Gain equaled success, loss equaled failure.

To his credit, for McGavran numbers were all about people.

Numbers of persons brought into living worshipping contact with the Way, the Truth, and the Life are never mere digits. They are always persons, beloved persons, persons for whom Christ died.

They are our own brothers and sisters. As such, the more who come to Christian faith the better. We consider any disparagement of "numbers" of converts ridiculous, and do not believe that on second thought many would advance the objection.[41]

But the troublesome implications of using a numbers-based accounting system are obvious. When numbers are what matter, to achieve numerical success is to gain a sense of well-being and confirmation in your ministry. It means that you are maximizing your resources and are focused on the mission of reaching the lost. It means that you will not see your resources transferred to other works. Numbers motivate you, generating a host of positive and negative responses.

The "Numerical Growth Principle" places a premium on success. There is nothing inherently wrong with that. The danger lies in how we gain the numbers. Are we truly developing numerical growth from the ground up, or are we cheating and stealing another's resources, calling them our own in an effort to enhance our performance stature? Obviously when numbers are a central criterion, the temptation to steal is very great.

Perhaps the worst generation that could have been presented with this criterion for measuring success was the baby boomers. "They're more entrepreneurial," notes Leith Anderson in *Dying for Change*. The generation is fascinated with numbers and success. One out of every two boomer families has investments in the stock market. Most have retirement accounts and are aggressively managing them. This generation developed Microsoft, the Internet and the metachurch. For them, numbers are a huge theological distraction because they become the measure of success. Yet numbers may not be an accurate tool to assess the spiritual development of people.

Church growth consultant George Barna is a baby boomer, and his approach exemplifies this generation's view of the church:

It is time, says Barna, for the church to adopt a whole new paradigm for understanding itself, a model borrowed from the contemporary business world. Like it or not, the church is not only in a market but is itself a business. It has a "product" to sell—relationships to Jesus and others; its "core product" is the message of salvation, and each local church is a "franchise." The church's pastors, says Barna, will be judged not by their teaching and counseling but by their ability to run the church "smoothly and efficiently" as if it were a business. And, like any secular business, the church must show a "profit," which is to say it must achieve success in penetrating and servicing its market.[42]

In other words, numbers really matter, often more than ethics, morals or biblical love.

McGavran developed all three of his principles with the best of intentions. These principles call Christians to take seriously the need to be productive and accountable stewards of the Lord's vineyard. Yet they served as springboards for unbiblical practices. These principles in fact inspire, justify and permanently sanction sheep stealing. They create an unbalanced formula for measuring kingdom growth, and they may have given birth to the stagnation trends in the church's current growth.

Who is the Good Shepherd? Following Jesus as a shepherd involves stewardship of resources, focus on the Master's commands and objectives, and a third quality that cannot be quantified: love for the people. Churches should be far more interested in helping each other grow and retain their members than gleefully stripping each other's membership rosters through transfer growth.

The Inner Examen

There is much good in the principles and methodologies of the Church Growth movement. However, sheep stealing highlights a perennial failure of the movement and the evangelical community in general. We habitually neglect to perform what is classically called the "inner examen." As described by Richard Foster, this involves reflection on the integrity of one's heart, character and practices, being sensitive to the Holy Spirit's counsel and instruction.

Such a process is imperative, especially for the church growth movement. By its nature the movement is constantly crossing orthodox boundaries of how we do church. Pushing the envelope places the movement in that dangerous vortex where newfound success can easily produce pride and warnings can be arrogantly ignored. If there has been one weakness in the church growth movement, it has been the high value we have placed on "being right."

If we do not become students of history we will be condemned to repeat it. That, in fact, is the case with our penchant for transfer growth. It has lured the church growth movement into the same flat conversion rates for which McGavran censured the Indian mission stations. Unless we identify and diagnose our own malaise, yet another movement of reform will replace us.

Chief among the errors is the church growth movement's response to the shocking lack of conversion growth. Just as the mission stations were discouraged by the slow advancement of the gospel in India, the church growth movement has been stymied by the relatively slow rate of conversions in church settings.

Slow Growth

Conversion growth, in general, graphs poorly. Even with the investment of considerable resources in evangelistic programs, conversion growth is slow growth. By its nature it requires the decision of one person at a time. Each of them needs to have the gospel presented in a fashion that they can understand, and often this requires the building of relational bridges to their world.

Rarely does one presentation of the gospel make sense to a person who does not know Christ; he or she needs to hear that message several times before responding. In the real world, evangelism never seems to develop that pyramidal marketing schematic of church growth seminars' flip charts. It is a time-consuming process.

Conversion growth actually can create a roadblock to fast

growth. When this is the case, we itch for other sources of growth. Biological growth—that is, the babies-build-the-church method—is also slow growth. Transfer growth, on the other hand, has few growth-inhibiting factors and offers the greatest potential for success. So it is ultimately where many pastors and churches actually place their efforts.

In an interview with a pastor of the largest church in his city, I inquired about the extraordinary growth the church was experiencing. "Oh yes, it is amazing," he replied. "We are busting at the seams here at First Church—our growth is over 150 percent this year alone. We have brought on a new pastor to the staff, and we have added a third service on Sunday mornings."

Then I asked, "How many baptisms have you had?"

Catching my drift, he estimated begrudgingly, "Oh, between thirty and forty." Those numbers, I thought, betrayed the source of growth for a church that has over eight hundred people as members.

Soon I interviewed another pastor from the same city. "Last year we had some challenges in our ministry," he confided. "One of the hardest things was losing over a dozen families to that huge First Church! It nearly killed us." This statement confirmed my suspicions: sheep stealing was one of First Church's primary means of growth.

In *Primary Purpose* Ted Haggard seems to sense the slippage in the church growth movement's focus. Haggard states that the church needs to be reoriented back toward the standard of conversion growth.

> The illusion of the past says, if my church is growing, then it is making a difference in our city. The reality is that if one life-giving church grows because another is declining, then there is no net difference in the social and cultural makeup of the city. Conversion growth is much more difficult, but it makes an immediate improvement in the water level of the Holy Spirit's activity in a city.[43]

The second lesson from history comes from McGavran's frustration over the churches' and mission boards' lack of concern about zero growth. Since the discovery of American churches' flat growth line in 1990, little has been done about it. In fact, new church growth materials continue to pour into the market—with one notable exception.[44] This violates a basic church growth rule: If something is not working, doing more of it, or doing it harder, will not help. To quote Albert Einstein, "You can not use the same kind of thinking to get out of a problem that you used when you got into it."

The solution, ironically, is the same one McGavran suggested for the problems in India over fifty years ago: gather empirical data and use the findings to correct the situation. There is one notable change that needs to take place regarding those statistics: we must understand the differences in the types of statistics that we collect and what it is that these statistics really mean.

Fatal Flaw

Statistics, like quotes, can be wildly misleading. If one fails to consider the context of a verse or of a person's statement, wrongful conclusions can be derived when we interpret what was said. The same is true when we interpret numbers. This was the church growth movement's fatal flaw. Increases in church size were misinterpreted as "mostly conversions" and "significant church growth" when in fact a heavy dependence on church transfers was actually occurring. In reality there were fewer conversions than perceived, and the neutralizing effects of recirculating the saints significantly offset actual growth in the universal body of Christ.

Failure to qualify the type of growth that increases the size of a given church seriously changes the interpretation of the significance of their evangelistic contribution. It is not correct to assess all growth equally. This is a common mistake that originates in the basic statistics that are used in church growth to determine an individual ministry's growth rate.

A prime example of this blindness can be seen in *The Church*

Growth Survey Handbook.[45] Here the standard church growth instructions are given on how to calculate your church's growth rate. To do so you are instructed to record a composite membership triangulation that includes the categories of church membership, worship attendance and adult Sunday school attendance. These figures are added together and then divided by three to create a "composite average." This average is then calculated for every week of the year, creating a "composite annual average." Now we have a figure that can be compared to other years to denote decline or increase in your church's growth. Typically, a ten-year period of time is used (it actually encompasses eleven years of data) to create what is known as a decadal growth rate.

This exercise does in fact accurately record a church's "numerical increase."[46] However, it is wrong to assume that this formula can be used to assess "kingdom growth," for extensive interchurch transfers would greatly affect "growth" statistics. The church growth movement simply never realized that church transfers was a category that needed to be included to validate the type of growth a church was experiencing.

It is ironic that the church growth movement, with its penchant for growth analysis, did not detect how quickly and significantly transfer growth was becoming the major contributing factor in the movement's growth statistics. Nothing could be more embarrassing.

The adverse effects of transfer growth also went undetected because church growth churches seem like they are engaging in mighty works. In church growth classes I saw chart after chart of graphs highlighting South American churches that were growing at astronomical rates. When we visited several southern California churches, we saw complexes that were the size of shopping malls. That these works might be failing to contribute to the kingdom count was not even a consideration. There was absolutely no perception of anything but monumental success from the movement's efforts. Blinded by the excitement of growth, we failed to grasp the bigger picture.

This still is an issue. When my fellow graduate students, most of them pastors, heard a presentation of my dissertation proposal, their responses were angry and anxious.

Many will argue that the studies' conclusions are wrong and that conversion growth is still the central goal of their own church's ministry. I will concede that the data are fresh and the concepts have not withstood prolonged and vigorous cross-examination. I hope such dialogue will occur. Nonetheless, if we have indeed allowed our primary focus to shift, it is vitally important to the movement and the kingdom of God that we recognize the trend and make appropriate kingdom-oriented adjustments.

Corrective Measures

The acknowledgment of different types of growth is an important first step in accurate assessment of a church's ministry. How else can you determine if your evangelistic outreach is effectively seeking the lost or merely attracting the already churched? If your use of statistics orients programming for your church and influences budget proposals, it is imperative that you understand what type of growth your ministry is effecting. To do that you need accurate data.

One of the steps we have taken in keeping better records of our growth has been through our accurate measurement of conversions. These are individuals who have been brought to a saving knowledge of Christ through the different ministries of our church. Annually we record these figures, providing for us a realistic picture of the "kingdom growth" that our church is actually engaged in.

We have benefited from this simple information, using it to influence the allocation of our resources to best promote our goal of leading people to Christ. We know that worship is important for conversions because we have information telling us that folks have come to faith through this ministry. This inspired us to purchase excellent sound equipment and to install a state-of-the-art projection system utilizing PowerPoint for all our sermons. Our audience uses these formats in their process of discovering God, and these investments have resulted in lives committed to Christ.

It also caused us to invest in youth ministries that are evangelistic in nature. In our case we developed a partnership with a parachurch organization called Young Life. Here we found a ministry that is very aggressive in reaching lost kids. Rather than investing in a traditional church youth group, we have invested our resources into Young Life in an effort to increase the "kingdom count" of teens in our city. Our money has been spent more effectively for the growth of God's kingdom as our youth group grows through genuine conversions, rather than through attracting kids from neighboring churches.

There are certainly other valid areas of ministry that any church may choose to focus their attention on. My point is that merely recording composite growth figures as a sign of your success or failure falls short of gathering information that accurately tells the story of your church's effectiveness. Ministry-specific data is far more valuable and needs to be developed by your specific church so that useful and correct interpretation of results can be made.

Numbers still play an important role in being able to determine the impact that a ministry is having in a give area. But they need to be the right numbers, and we must seek to utilize them as tools of assessing where the Spirit of God would have us keep in step with his work.

Conclusion

In chapter four we have uncovered a startling fact: during the decades in which church growth principles have been applied most widely, the church has been in a serious state of decline. That seems impossible given the vast array of new church growth strategies and programs that have been employed. What possible explanation could there be to account for this shocking news?

I have proposed the hypothesis that the church growth movement was focusing on something other than conversion growth, something that would consume our efforts and resources but not make a difference in the Christian population base in the world. That something was numerical success. In achieving this goal we engaged aggressively in transfer growth which produced for us the numbers we wanted, but also caused the church to wander away from the tougher conversion growth practices. This has created the declining trends in evangelical populations that we are experiencing today.

To establish this theory, we looked at two classic church growth settings in the United States and an exhaustive research project carried out by the church in Australia. My personal research has included interviews with pastors from all over the United States, Nigeria and Mexico. In all of these settings, the trend of high transfer growth practices is strongly established.

Chapter four also spent some time discovering why the church growth movement actually seems to support sheep stealing in many of its methodologies. Here we examined Donald McGavran's book *The Bridges of God* and found several principles that originally attempted to make evangelistic efforts amongst ministries more effective but in the end were transformed by the church growth movement into principles that allowed transfer growth practices to flourish.

We ended the chapter with an affirming concept: good data can produce good insights into how we allocate the resources of our ministries. With this type of information it is possible for churches to become genuinely successful in the areas of ministry to which God has called them.

PART 3

5

Fleecing the Flock

The thief comes only to steal and kill and destroy;
I have come that they may have life, and have it to the full.
I am the good shepherd. The good shepherd lays down his life
for the sheep. The hired hand is not the shepherd who owns
the sheep. So when he sees the wolf coming,
he abandons the sheep and runs away. Then the wolf attacks
the flock and scatters it. The man runs away because
he is a hired hand and cares nothing for the sheep.
JOHN 10:10-13

Many things come with hidden costs. Purchase a new car and you will be presented with expenses that go well beyond the sticker price—such things as sales taxes, excise taxes, dealer destination charges, registration fees, town taxes, insurance premiums.

Stealing sheep, too, comes with hidden costs. Over the years that I have been studying its effects on the church, I have been amazed at how extensive its hidden deviltry is. The transferring of a church membership is simply the surface issue. Transfer growth has costs, hidden costs that greatly affect all who are part of its processes.

The hidden costs of transfer growth, the adverse effects of this practice on the entire kingdom of God, will be exposed in this chapter. There are seven deadly sins that are the ensigns of transfer growth. Each will be fully explored to uncover its impact on the church and its destructive nature. Hopefully, by studying transfer growth each of us in ministry will develop a new respect for the inherent dangers of this process and a new resolve to eradicate it from our midst.

The Seven Deadly Sins

The first deadly sin that we will examine is the crippling of churches. Sheep stealing has the potential to greatly affect the health of smaller churches, either killing them through extensive transfer decline or permanently crippling the church's ability to engage in a mission.

In recent years the trend toward larger church settings that provide a broad range of services has greatly threatened the existence of smaller neighborhood churches. We often hear glorious stories about large churches that have grown at impressive rates of speed, but rarely do we hear about the smaller churches whose pews were drained.

One of the church growth movement's most recent success stories is the New Life Church in Colorado Springs, whose pastor, Ted Haggard, is committed to conversion growth in his ministry. Pastor Haggard estimates that in spite of New Life's best efforts not to engage in transfer growth, roughly fifty percent of his congregation is drawn from the pews of other churches.[1]

The math on that statistic creates a startling picture. According to their website, New Life Church has a worship attendance of roughly seven thousand people. If fifty percent of their membership is comprised of transfers, that means that thirty-five hundred people came from other ministry settings. What kind of impact does this type of transfer growth have on other churches in the community?

Kennon Callahan, in his book *Twelve Keys to an Effective Church*, states that to gain a realistic assessment of your church's stature you should compare the size of your church to a national average to determine how large your ministry really is. Using a chart developed by the department of statistics of the Methodist denomination, Callahan notes that a church with one hundred people in attendance at their worship service is in the eighty-second percentile for church size. This qualifies as a large church setting in this denomination, and as Callahan points out, these statistics are basically the same for many other Protestant denominations.[2]

To create a ministry the size of New Life Church required transferring the equivalent of thirty-five large churches into that setting. The impact on the churches in the Colorado Springs community must have been significant. Granted, some of the churches that lost members were perhaps places where transferring out was a healthy step,[3] but surely even solid Christ-centered churches were affected by the "growth" of New Life Church.[4]

The creating of megachurches at the expense of smaller churches is much like the phenomenon one witnesses when a large supermarket opens in a small community. Soon all the mom-and-pop stores where everyone is known on a first-name basis and where your credit is good are gone. There is a similar sense of loss when small churches disappear. For many the intimate size of a smaller congregation is desirable. This is especially true today as we see people seeking to find places of meaning and intimacy to combat the sterile largeness of the rest of their lives.

Small groups are, in effect, the large church's answer to the issue of intimacy. There is, however, a value in a small church that can not be reproduced in small group settings: having a personal relationship with a pastor, instead of just seeing a video projection image of a church CEO; being part of a small environment where you have to be involved; enjoying a sense of success on a grassroots level as the church celebrates conversions or engages in modest but all-consuming outreach ministries. It is the value of having a place where you sincerely have a sense of ownership and a civic pride in your church's contribution to the community.

I fear that the verdict is still out regarding the overall impact that the loss of the small church will have on the Christian community as a whole. My sense is that we need these elements of the body, and their demise, especially through transfer growth, is regrettable.

How can this trend be reversed? Perhaps the two greatest mistakes of small churches being threatened by other ministries are underestimating their value and failing to branch out into new ministry growth opportunities.

Small churches that underestimate their value often tend to not see what it is that they are very good at and focus harshly on trying to obtain all the ministry items that they do not possess. Recently I spoke with a pastor who has a church that is rich in ethnic heritage and a congregation that is fluent in the orthodox tenets of the faith and covenant theology. His parishioners, though modest in numbers, are neat people.

Their church is a very stable environment. In a day and age when many churches are scrambling to pay the mortgage every month, these folks have long since cleared the debt and are investing their money admirably in kingdom ministries. Their church is on a prime piece of real estate and has very high visibility. Yet this congregation struggles with their image and feels that they have little to offer people compared to other larger churches in our community.

In a world where people have been rejected and where God is an unknown commodity, this church is an oasis in the desert of life! Seizing your church's strengths and using them are often the keys to success. Certainly there are always programs or items that need to be added to every church's structure just as a matter of staying current, but do not despise the five little stones you have in your bag with your slingshot. The Lord is sovereign, and often your small offerings are just the right tools for the mission that the Lord has for you. Be faithful in the little things, and be bold in your expectations of the gifts that you do have.

There are some simple steps that this small church is taking that will change their ministry. First, they are tapping into the strong theological training of their congregation. These folks know the Scriptures and have a solid sense of systematic theology. What they lacked was a format to use these tools for the kingdom. By inspiring and training the congregation to engage in evangelism, they began to catch a vision for their potential. In this case the Alpha series was introduced to the church as a vehicle to help them reach out to people in the community who were looking for answers. This experience is leading the church into long-term mentoring programs and into exploring other ways that they can invest their "stones" into the community. In short, their strength is being honed, and they are providing solid evangelical discipleship to new believers.

Small churches can also fall victim to sheep stealing due to their lack of programs. Large churches often can provide better programming for their congregations, tempting your sheep to wander. This is perhaps one of the greatest struggles for the small church, for people have become used to expecting unlimited options for their wants and needs. Here the strength of the small church is mobility and flexibility.

New Englanders are notoriously creative! They are inventive, frugal and able to horse trade with the best of them. They also possess another quality that is the key to the success of the small church—they share resources.

Churches that learn to share their programs with other ministries in their community gain the advantage of tapping into a host of resources that can satisfy the needs of the people in their congregations. But to accomplish this, the fear of sheep stealing must be put to rest. Churches must learn to trust one another and actually be in the spirit of rejoicing when others succeed. Learning to utilize the broader range of gifts and talents that are available in the universal body of Christ spells success for the small church and greatly complements the quality of the small church experience.

Related to sharing resources is the need for the small church to try new things. Modernity is a serious issue that needs to be wisely discerned in each church setting, but there are so many productive ministries and programs to explore that are positive and will richly bless the lives of your people. Explore growth opportunities and expand your thinking outside of your comfort zone.

Remember much transfer growth occurs because of a church's hard heart toward trying something new. Parishioners become frustrated and feel uncared for when boards, consistories, deaconates, elders or pastors automatically dismiss any change. There is a famous slogan among church growth pastors that captures the results of such an attitude. They are called the seven last words of a church: "We've never done it that way before."

Change is challenging, but to grow into ministries or programming that is reasonable for your church and desired by your membership is good shepherding. People who are part of a church that is sincere in being genuine and willing to stretch to meet their needs will often be loyal to that body.

Small churches possess one other strength that they must utilize when they are being oppressed by transfer decline. Because of their size and intimacy they often have very strong relational ties to each other, reflecting the words of 1 Peter 1:22-23: "Now that you have purified yourselves by obeying the truth so that you have sincere love for your brothers, love one another deeply, from the heart. For you have been born again, not of perishable seed, but of imperishable, through the living and enduring word of God." When transfer decline appears, do not make the mistake of just letting people slip away; use these strong ties and simply confront the issue head on.

Several times in my ministry I have visited parishioners who had started to attend other churches. I was honest with them, sharing that it really hurt our community in many ways to lose them. We were sincere in expressing that whatever their concerns were, we wanted to grow together in Christ to overcome those issues. God speaks through the body, and perhaps God was using them to help us become aware of this concern for the good of his kingdom. We needed them; they were part of our body, and we did not want to see them go. Many times these brothers and sisters have returned to the church.

There is a current trend in America toward lifestyles that reflect the values of yesterday. The Beatles are back at the top of the record, or I should say, CD charts. Detroit is producing cars that resemble the roadsters of the past, and the clothes in the attic are being worn by my teenager. I suspect that the small church may well experience a renaissance in the days ahead. Small churches may never ride the crest of the numerical success wave, but they may well be instrumental in mentoring the next Billy Graham as they bring a quality to the Christian experience that is often lost in the shuffle of size.

Crippling churches through extensive transfer decline is impacting the overall well being of the body of Christ. This is an area that merits further study, for we would do well to consider the long-term effects of our "church growth" actions. Harming the bride of Christ remains the number one sin of sheep stealing.

Killing Church Leaders

The second deadly sin of transfer growth strikes the leadership of the church. Transfer growth can kill church leaders, robbing them of their vision, passion and love of church ministry. This is yet another hidden cost of the widely accepted practice of transferring church memberships.

There are few conversations more depressing than those of a church leader with a parishioner who is transferring membership to another church. No matter what the motivations or how logical the reasoning; often it still feels like personal rejection to the shepherd. Why does it hurt so much? Beyond the disappointment of having a declining membership list, there were three dominant themes that kept appearing in the interviews I did with pastors on this subject.

The investment factor. Professional clergy invest in people's lives. They spend hours counseling and visiting, forming deep spiritual attachments to the people to whom they believe God wants them to minister. In return, they hope for commitment. Right or wrong, it is an expectation that even the apostle Paul acknowledged.[5]

Ironically, often the parishioner that requires the largest investment of a pastor's time and energy is also the one who is prone to wander. The resulting resentment of being used is a temptation that often assaults overtaxed clergy.

Brent and Lois were a struggling couple. Brent suffered from bouts of depression and sometimes treated Lois abusively. His fixation on pornography steadily drove a wedge between him and Lois. Pastor Davis took Brent under his wing, spending hours counseling, listening and dropping by Brent's home to be his friend.

When Brent needed a new job, Pastor Davis used church connections to help him out. During a flood, the pastor bought a kerosene heater and delivered it to the family's house. When Lois's father had a heart attack, Pastor Davis was the first concerned friend at the hospital. When Brent's mother in Chicago was sick, Pastor Davis sent her flowers and a note of encouragement.

One day Lois arrived at the church with the kids. Bus tickets in hand, she was leaving Brent because he had been sliding back into his old ways. Once again Pastor Davis used his skills and dedication to help the family through those dark days.

One Sunday Pastor Davis heard through the grapevine that Brent and Lois were attending a new church plant near their home. "It just killed me," said the pastor. "I thought that we were closer than that. It makes me feel like what I do is perceived by people as just a job. It is not. I pour my life and soul into people, and trite commitment like theirs makes me want to just quit making this investment. Nobody cares about the church. Everybody is in it for themselves. It's hard not to be cynical when you feel like ministry is this long, narrow, one-way street."

Sometimes church hopping is pathological. Sometimes church leaders accurately identify the stumbling blocks in people's lives for which they have been seeking help, and they panic at the thought of now having to deal with them. Suddenly a new environment where nobody knows them, and where they will not be held accountable, becomes very appealing. Having worked hard to help people grow and overcome the things that keep them from wholeness, pastors become deeply discouraged to see such folks leave their church for another—only to backslide.

Roxanne and Ty were relatively new arrivals at the Essex Episcopal Church. One night the church's small groups' director visited their home and Roxanne made inappropriate advances toward him. Other members of the pastoral staff were distressed to learn of the incident, but fortunately this was a healthy church and her actions were not simply dismissed.

"We got Ty and Roxanne right into counseling," said Father Tom. "Stuff was real thick; Roxanne and Ty had had this problem before. They said that they thought a move would help them—and that Roxanne's promiscuity was over with now. I should have picked up on that warning sign. In the end Ty enabled her to avoid the church's discipline, accountability and oversight by going to another church that she begged him to try out. She was just running. I believe their move cost Ty his marriage. They are divorced today."

Father Tom continued: "You asked me about hidden costs. Well, other than the obvious outcome of Roxanne's marriage I have a pastoral staff that was very angry and depressed about the way Ty enabled his wife. It took a lot out of us, and understandably they are reluctant to jump right into a situation like that again."

The men and women who pick up the mantle of shepherding God's flock invest their lives into people and often pay a heavy price. When we allow transfer growth to flow unchecked, we are hurting God's anointed, thereby weakening the flock. These are real costs for the kingdom.

Hard hearts. A second serious hidden cost for pastors is hard hearts. As a result of the pain of rejection and emotional abuse, many pastors who were open and giving at the inception of their ministry begin a gradual shift into what they see as self-preservation. When clergy have suffered a history of rejection through transfer loss, it is easy for them to become cynical about the people they serve. "The church loves a minister who is on fire," commented an Assembly of God pastor. "They will sit for hours and watch him burn!"

This pain can create a wall between the clergy and the people, as pastors insulate themselves from getting too close to the ones they serve. In the end it leads to a professional atmosphere more like a medical clinic than a church. Problems are dealt with, but personal attachment is avoided. "The phrase 'heart of a pastor,'" writes David Goetz, "has lost much of its currency."[6]

The killing of a pastor's heart for the ministry can lead to a serious loss of integrity. Over time, Sunday after Sunday, pastors face the vexing problem of preaching what they are no longer willing to do. "How can I speak of small groups and trusting one another," lamented my Baptist brother, "when I do not trust people—and would never be caught dead in a small group because of that!" The church is affected by the loss of leadership by example—and many pastors begin to feel the pangs of depression as they sense the dichotomy of living lies.

Loss of mission. Finally, the cold metal of rejection severs the legs of a pastor's vision and mission. To be about a mission, to have people rally around that cause, gives life and inspiration to the task of pastoring. Conversely, abandonment is the loneliest form of rejection. "Even if all fall away on account of you, I never will" (Mt 26:33). "I don't know the man!" (Mt 26:72). How much darker did the hour of trial become for Jesus with Peter's betrayal!

Recreational church-hoppers, people who flit in and out of churches, usually gain entry into the pastor's heart by generating tons of enthusiasm and goodwill. "This church is so wonderful;

Pastor, your sermons are so powerful," they gush. Sometimes they jump into the ministry, get the pastor and the church's resources committed to new programs, and then suddenly disappear, crippling the church with the pain of rejection and the false start of new ministries.

Pastor Jordan told me about what he called his "Amway Experience." "One Sunday morning we had an entire group of Amway distributors walk through the door of our church. There must have been fifteen of them or so, and they were wonderful people. Our offerings jumped by almost one thousand dollars per week! I pretty much knew it had to be their contributions that were making the difference.

"After about a month of steady attendance, members of this group began to get involved in the church. They stretched us to make some bold moves for our church, and the new energy was refreshing. Just as I was starting to think that the church might be on the verge of something big—they left! I mean they all left, en masse. Bill, I tell you I never saw such a thing. One Sunday they were here, the next they were gone.

"I called and asked what had happened, and nothing was wrong; they were just attending another church now to help that one grow! Well, our church was left dumbfounded. We were overcommitted and over budget, and I was in some hot water. If they thought that they were helping me by getting my hopes up and then leaving, well, they were wrong. Oh, that was depressing."

Being left for greener pastures hurts. Zeal and inspiration can be, and are, rent from the heart of leaders who endure such abuse. The resulting pain has helped give the ministry one of the highest dropout rates of any profession.

In the superintendent's report of an annual meeting of the Advent Christian denomination, the following statistics were cited from the National Clergy Support Network.[7]

Eighty percent of the pastors surveyed believe that pastoral ministry has negatively affected their families. Seventy percent of all pastors

surveyed do not have someone in their congregation that they consider a close friend. Fifty percent of the test group has considered
leaving the ministry in the past three months. Fifty percent of all
ministers who go into full-time service drop out after five years.
Fifty percent of those who remain in ministry beyond five years will
eventually burn out and leave the ministry permanently. Thirteen
hundred pastors are forcibly terminated from their charges—each
month.[8]

The sad fact is that many of the servants of the cross are taken out
by friendly fire. As one pastor put it, "I don't mind taking an arrow
in my chest as I lead the church into the battle with the enemy. It's
the arrows in my back that kill me."

Pastors who support and participate in transfer growth are part
of the problem. Thus if you are a pastor, the next time you receive
visitors from a sister church you would do well to consider this
regarding the pastor whose church these people have just left:

☐ Almost all clergy have had specialized training.
☐ Many have completed college.
☐ A majority hold at least a master's degree.
☐ Some have gone on for postgraduate degrees.
☐ All made large career sacrifices to become a pastor.
☐ Most could make far more money in another job.
☐ Many live sacrificially to do what they are doing.
☐ Most fasted and prayed about the church they went to.
☐ Most felt called by God to that position.
☐ Daily they carry more burdens than the world will ever know.

The world is not worthy of them, and you invalidate them if
you assume that you have the right to take, at your leisure, any
one of the people whom God called, trained, prepared and
ordained them to care for. That's a bold move.

Although sheep stealing is only one of many reasons that pastors are leaving the ministry, I believe it to be a significant factor.
Nothing erodes pastors' self-esteem or challenges their call more
quickly than the loss of members from their charge. Satan glories
in the pastoral killing fields created by transfer growth.

Loss of an Ecumenical Spirit

The third deadly sin is the loss of the ecumenical spirit of the kingdom of God. Some see this as a good thing![9] Separatists have long feared the watering down of the gospel that occurs when liberals and conservatives attempt to accomplish a common goal. But this is not what I am referring to. I am addressing the loss of trust between evangelical conservative churches. This loss is a direct byproduct of transfer growth.

As a young pastor, I asked an older Congregational pastor in our town if he would mentor me. I was unprepared for his cold response. "What," he replied, "and have you steal the rest of my congregation?"

I was pretty naive about the impact a few transfers had had on our relationship. Resentment, distrust and ultimately the severing of our united evangelical front would be the fruits of those transgressions.

Transfer growth makes posting another church's special events difficult. There is a latent fear that when our people see another church's wares—their building, property, wonderful choir, pastor—they will choose to leave our church. Such insecurity is often well founded. People love to wander, and the latest and greatest seems to possess an irresistible draw.

This seldom-acknowledged fear divides the strength of the body. Churches politely coexist with each other, but maintain safeguards that greatly limit their corporate involvement. Turf guarding becomes Pastoral Ministry 101 as soon as you experience the negative flow of the circulation of the saints.

What does that do to the kingdom? Think about it: "Every kingdom divided against itself will be ruined, and every city or household divided against itself will not stand" (Mt 12:25). If we are constantly at risk of being hurt or robbed when we are together, then we will have no desire for ecclesiastical communion. Our distrust of each other condemns each church to become an island unto itself. Each ministry has its own programs, often duplicating

others' efforts. In this fashion countless kingdom dollars are squandered. How delighted the dark side must be with the disdain we
have for each other.

Donald G. Bloesch captures God's vision for what the church
should look like: "The goal of authentic ecumenism is not a super-
church with power and prestige but rather a worldwide fellowship
of believers united under the Word and dedicated to the conversion and salvation of mankind. What we should aim for is . . . an
evangelical ecumenism which places Christian mission above institutional survival."[10]

We should have unity, but it is impossible for us to present the
united front the New Testament portrays for the church until we
can trust one another. That means living together in unity. Francis
Schaeffer has called this "the orthodoxy of community"—that is,
the straightness of living together. The picture is expanded by
D. James Kennedy:

> The loving unity of God's people, living in a disciplined relationship
> with each other under the authority and the love of God, becomes a
> demonstration to the world of the power and the truth of the gos-
> pel. Though the precepts of the gospel may be proclaimed to an
> individual in a few minutes, their reality must be lived out in a life-
> time of relationship within the body of Christ. This has properly
> been called body evangelism.[11]

"The church being one in Christ as Christ is one in the Father
certainly means more than mere doctrinal agreement. The cross
must be taken as the basis of not only soteriology but of ethics as
well,"[12] urges Howard Snyder. How do we learn to love and build
up each other as our congregations seek numerical growth? And
what are good biblical standards for wandering sheep?

Loss of Biblical Morality

The fourth deadly sin of sheep stealing is a loss of biblical morality. Compromise is the death of virtue. The desire to grow our own
churches at the expense of all other concerns has prompted some

unpleasant trend-setting methodologies and standards within the church growth movement.

The death of morals can be seen in compromising church growth slogans like "Fat sheep don't wander." The truth is that all sheep can wander. That is why the Bible instructs us to return them.

> If you see your brother's ox or sheep straying, do not ignore it but be sure to take it back to him. If the brother does not live near you or if you do not know who he is, take it home with you and keep it until he comes looking for it. Then give it back to him. Do the same if you find . . . anything [your brother] loses. Do not ignore it. (Deut 22:1-3)

Church members are of course not property, but the intent of the ethics behind those verses is appropriate. There is an obligation to protect the interest of your brother or sister.

Stealing sheep has been justified using axioms such as "The end justifies the means."[13] The Word of God is in constant tension with such a philosophy; justifying our numerical success often requires serious bending of the Scriptures. We begin calling wrong right when we justify any action that secures for us the results that we desire.

In a council of hell's denizens, the experienced devil Screwtape rises to argue:

> They do not understand either the source or the real character of the prohibitions they are breaking. Their consciousness hardly exists apart from the social atmosphere that surrounds them. And of course we have contrived that their very language should be all smudge and blur; what would be a bribe in someone else's profession is a tip or a present in theirs. The job of their tempters was first, of course, to harden these choices of hellward roads into a steady repetition. But then (and this was all-important) to turn the habit into a principle—a principle the creature is prepared to defend. After that—all will go well.[14]

Concerned about the advancement of this secular attitude,

David Wells writes:

> The church is paying a high price for all of this success. When success is purchased by setting aside the truth of God, by dabbling in ecclesiastical engineering that is open to all that is new and experimental and closed to what is fixed and eternal, when it involves transforming spirituality into organization, the pastor into a business executive, and genuine Christian hope into churchly amusement and fraternity—then it is putting the evangelical soul at grave risk.[15]

The Methods of Modernity

Several significant books warn of the perils of applying certain methods of modernity to the way we do church: Douglas D. Webster's *Selling Jesus* (InterVarsity Press, 1992), Os Guinness's *Dining with the Devil* (Baker, 1993), David Wells's *God in the Wasteland* (Eerdmans, 1994), Marva J. Dawn's *Reaching Out Without Dumbing Down: A Theology of Worship for the Turn-of-the-Century Culture* (Eerdmans, 1995) and Philip Kenneson and James Street's *Selling Out the Church* (Abingdon, 1997).

Growing the church can be reduced to running a business. "How else," writes Guinness, "can you explain the comment of a Japanese businessman to a visiting Australian? 'Whenever I meet a Buddhist leader, I meet a holy man. Whenever I meet a Christian leader, I meet a manager.'"[16] A secular-to-ecclesiastical assimilation is moving the church toward a capitalistic theology in which numerical and financial success has become the standard at the expense of ethics, biblical theology and moral values.

"He who sups with the devil had better have a long spoon. The devilry of modernity has its own magic," warns Peter Berger. "The [believer] who sups with it will find his spoon getting shorter and shorter—until that last supper in which he is left alone at the table, with no spoon at all and with an empty plate. The devil, one may guess, will by then have gone away to more interesting company."[17]

The most incriminating evidence of the shifting values of the church growth movement comes from the movement itself. The often-quoted axiom "The end justifies the means" does not actually reflect the values of the person who first applied that principle to church growth. C. Peter Wagner's original statement was "The End Justifies the Means—as long as it is moral."[18]

To illustrate how that is applied, Wagner quoted Paul: "To the weak I became weak, to win the weak. I have become all things to all men so that by all possible means I might save some" (1 Cor 9:22). Paul's point, and Wagner's, had to do with earning the right to be heard so that the gospel can be presented—not with raiding another church so that one's own church can grow.

It is a dangerous line. Like many other church growth principles, what was intended for good became twisted, propelled by numerical success, and changed its nature. At such points the church growth movement's principles have flown into the arms of modernity.

> Modernity is in many ways giving contemporary expression to what the New Testament pejoratively calls "the world." Worldliness is that system of values, in any given age, which has at its center our fallen human perspective, which displaces God and his truth from the world, and which makes sin look normal and righteousness seem strange. It thus gives great plausibility to what is morally wrong and, for that reason, makes what is wrong seem normal. It is this spiritual reality that is pervasive in modernity and that has caused the evangelical world to stumble badly.[19]

Ends-justifying-means modernity brings hard-line, cutthroat business practices into the church, damaging the body of Christ.

"The man just ate me for lunch." I could see the hurt and frustration as Clayton told me his story. "Skip was our worship leader. When he and his family showed up, I was at a point of needing some encouragement. I had no doubt that God sent them. They were an answer to my prayers. Once Skip came on board, things were really coming together. I poured my life into Skip, and God blessed him and our church. Pretty soon we had a few new families attending our worship service—and then the Christian Center fellowship stole him."

"What do you mean by that?" I asked.

"They needed a worship leader, so they contacted Skip. They wined and dined him and his wife and offered him a salaried position. We could not afford to match their offer. Skip is a good guy, but he wanted to get into ministry and the offer was just too good. I called up the pastor to talk with him about my concerns about his brazen stripping of our staff, and he blew me off. Oh, he listened politely and then just said the decision was up to Skip. What decision? We had nothing to offer."

What are our moral obligations when it comes to the topic of transfer growth? According to Gene A. Getz:

> The greatest moral standard is love. Foundational to all meaningful Christian action is love. It is the "more excellent way" (1 Corinthians 12:31; 13:13). And as might be expected, the exhortation to "love one another" appears more frequently than all others. Of the 48 references to what we are to do for one another as fellow believers, 11 times we are told to love one another. If you add Christ's direct commands to "love one another" which are recorded in John's Gospel, the total comes to 16 in the New Testament. There is no question as to what is most important. Love is the greatest! To love fellow believers is a basic injunction of the New Testament—repeated more than any other.[20]

Love builds up. Anything less and should be avoided at all costs.

A friend of mine is an Orthodox priest. His tradition is not generally at home in the church growth movement or the evangelical community. "I cannot meet the needs of our young families," he lamented. "Your church has it all. You've got music, energy and small groups. What do I have? I have nothing."

Stealing Constantine's sheep would have certainly been possible. My wife and I had relationships with several parishioners in his church. Instead, because of my convictions about transfer growth, I offered this man another option. "Why don't you and your wife join our small group for a year? You can learn how it is done and take that experience back to your people."

He was shocked, but they did it! Now his church can not only offer its rich traditions of faith but also meet the needs of our relationship-starved society. We see each other often and love each other deeply. His words to me embrace the morals of good growth, "You are a good friend."[21]

Much more could be, and eventually needs to be, written regarding morals and church growth, but two basic principles should be articulated right now. First, pastors who know Christ and churches that preach Christ are all the body of Christ[22]; it is not just about one's own church. How you grow matters. Any violation of love by expanding one's church at the expense of another must be considered a violation of moral integrity.

Second, to violate the first principle is to distance oneself from the Holy Spirit. When we become void of his energy and empty of his power, the place we call church becomes just a faint image of what it was intended to be. "Do not grieve the Holy Spirit," writes Paul (Eph 4:30), for in so doing we abandon a Christ-centered vision and stray into a world of self-centered standards.

Denial of Conflict

The fifth deadly sin is denial of conflict. Transfer growth creates a tempting easy out for those confronted by conflict. Rather than dealing with difficult issues and resolving the situation, they choose the nonconfrontational option of fleeing. When conflicts are addressed through escape, the church suffers many negative effects.

The biblical writers were not afraid of conflict; in fact they demonstrate acute awareness of the tensions that exist within God's people. Scripture's primary concern is to open up the pain caused by conflict and resolve the issues.

Paul notes that a person can harbor hurt for only a few hours before it becomes a seed for satanic influence in the soul. "Do not let the sun go down while you are still angry, and do not give the devil a foothold" (Eph 4:26-27). This speaks of the progressive nature of sin. Once we are wounded, if we do not release the spiritual hurt of the wound, it becomes internalized. External wounds hurt, but internal wounds are often fatal as the infection of sin overcomes other parts of our spiritual body.

Hate, anger and malice are all signs of discord (see Jas 4:1-4), and all of them lead to death (Rom 6:23). Not addressing conflict or pain creates a victim, and a victim's mentality fosters growing paranoia. This is one of the most common kinds of church transferees: someone who has been hurt and is fleeing the source of the pain. The best thing you could ever do for their spiritual well-being is send them back to resolve the conflict.

Christians are not reborn with a capacity for disharmony and division. When we are separated by conflict, we are robbed of our security and joy. To use escape as a way of resolving problems is to scratch an indelible line in our spirit where our growth is arrested. We travel no further; we gain no higher ground. This line defines the end of our spiritual leash and has created a generation of victims tethered to their worst fears.

I am not ignorant of the abuses that can exist in churches. That is why Christ gives clear instructions about how to confront conflict.

> If your brother sins against you, go and show him his fault, just between the two of you. If he listens to you, you have won your brother over. But if he will not listen, take one or two others along, so that "every matter may be established by the testimony of two or three witnesses." If he refuses to listen to them, tell it to the church; and if he refuses to listen even to the church, treat him as you would a pagan or a tax collector. (Mt 18:15-17)

These guidelines include a safeguard that allows wrongs to be challenged. Even a pastor or elder can be challenged (1 Tim 5:19) for the sake of his or her spiritual growth and harmony.

Denial of conflict in the church has created a generation of Christians addicted to therapeutic ministries. Healing sells hot.

Books that offer a promise of wholeness burn off the shelves of Christian bookstores.

Instead of viewing conflict as a tool for growth, most Christians are afraid of it. This fear of pain creates an emotional isolationist mentality in the church. We begin to walk alone, struggling not to need others. In the words of Matthew Arnold, "In the sea of life . . . we mortal millions live alone."[23]

How much has escapism actually affected the church?

> No one knows how many other people across the country have followed a similar pattern [of] enthusiastic involvement in a fellowship of believers, followed by a period of conflicts that are never quite resolved, leading to a crisis in which the decision is made to leave and finally a quiet exit—sometimes to another church, as often as not to no other church. I would put the number in the hundreds of thousands, if not in the millions. Whatever the total, I believe it is growing.[24]

Escapees affect the church not only by hopping around but by choosing to divorce themselves from the body—the ultimate form of transfer growth as the devil gains a convert.

Living with pain, living alone, divorces us from Christ's richest gifts of wholeness and community. It changes the gospel, destroys its promise and leaves us living a lie. Separatism is not Christianity, for as Dietrich Bonhoeffer once wrote, "it is impossible to experience Christianity outside of community."[25]

Why is that true? We need interaction with people to understand the cross. Escapism allows us to call ourselves Christians without the testing of our resolve. Instead of practicing core biblical principles such as forgiveness, reconciliation, servanthood, humility, longsuffering, perseverance and love, we simply hop to another setting. This creates cheap grace: we think that belief in doctrines without any effort on our part will save us.[26]

Enabled by transfer growth practices, we embrace an effortless, sugarcoated, have-it-your-way faith. Circumventing the cross of Christ, cheap grace is only a hollow form of Christianity with no understanding of the Spirit's regenerative power. It tries to cling to salvation while condemning others, judges while it asks not to be judged, and practices a form of murder as people are simply removed from one's life, annihilated.

In Scripture, being corrected is never something to be despised. It always hurts at first, but in the end it yields spiritual fruit. If we fail to confront, then we empower the dark side to slowly dominate our brother or sister. If we check them, challenge them, then there is the opportunity for spiritual growth (Jas 5:19-20).

Throughout the New Testament we often see Paul challenging individuals, churches and Christian leaders in regard to their faith and practices. His motivation was to bring them into conformity with the Spirit of Christ. James Dobson calls this tough love[27]—a love that does not allow evil to rule anymore.

As ministers of the gospel of Jesus Christ, we need to create an environment where church discipline, or at least dialogue, can be established. Too many times people just leave. No discussion, no understanding of their pain—they just leave. When such wounded people wish to transfer into our church, helping them to confront their conflict is often the right thing to do.

My wife Carol and I were at a Steve Green concert in Portland. As we walked down the aisle, a man I had never met addressed me: "Pastor Chadwick, isn't it?" For a moment I wondered if I should admit to being him. "You don't know me; I'm Charlie Scott. I'm a deacon at South Church, and I just wanted to thank you for sending Jack and Cathy Pratt back to talk to us."

Suddenly I understood. Cathy and Jack had attended my church for about a month before I had a chance to invite them to my study. There I asked them about their church experiences. Jack quickly explained that they had had a falling-out at their home church and "were in the market" for a new one. It was a new church growth moment—an opportunity to build the body of Christ.

I encouraged Jack and Cathy to go back to their "home" church. They were initially pretty surprised by my apparent rejection of

them, but I began articulating my convictions about the importance of the body of Christ and the need to experience confession,
forgiveness and reconciliation.

Evidently they had followed through. "When Jack and Cathy
called to talk to us, it was a real blessing. Those kids had grown
up in our church. We'd had a misunderstanding, but it all worked
out. Thank you, pastor, for your investment in our church."

Domestication of the Evangelistic Spirit

The sixth deadly sin is the domestication of the church's evangelistic spirit. The church growth movement was launched out of passion for reaching the lost. "The overall purpose of God for the
unsaved people of the world is basic to New Testament Christianity and also to church growth. 'The Son of Man is come to seek
and save that which was lost' (Luke 19:10)."[28] This was Donald
McGavran's consuming passion,[29] to unleash the resources of
Christ's church in a press for world evangelization. "In spite of all,
. . . according to the Bible, one task is paramount. Today's
supreme task is the effective multiplication of churches in the
receptive societies of the earth."[30]

"God searches until He finds. He searches where He finds. He
reconciles people to Himself. He has appointed us shepherds. He
commands us to find and save the lost!"[31]

This philosophy of ministry was also articulated in *The Master's
Plan for Making Disciples*, by church growth consultants Win and
Charles Arn:

> Being [Christ's] follower assumed not only an active commitment to
> His Lordship, but also included active involvement in the propaga-
> tion of His Gospel. By definition disciples became "fishers of men."
> Christ's central desire for His disciples was that when He was gone
> they would have ingrained in their hearts and minds the conviction
> that the Son of Man had come to seek and to save those who were
> lost. . . . He endeavored to make the matter as simple and easy to
> understand as possible . . . "go and make disciples."[32]

Make no mistake about it. The church growth movement had one focus: conversion growth. Leading people to a saving knowledge of Jesus Christ was the founders' expressed and theologically sound objective. Then came the news of 1991—*no growth* in the evangelical church for the previous ten years. So what happened? Transfer growth—churches had discovered an easy way to grow.

In Yellowstone National Park, Park Services staff dread receiving the report of a mauling. When a grizzly bear or a mountain lion discovers how easy it is to catch and kill a domestic animal, they lose their desire to hunt anything else. Which would you choose: chasing elk at breakneck speed, splashing through icy currents in hopes of catching a salmon, or overpowering a docile sheep or steer with a fraction of the effort?

Transfer growth develops a taste in the church for domestic stock. The hard work of earning the right to be heard, incarnational evangelism and explaining the Four Spiritual Laws or the bridge diagram is like chasing that elk. It's tough, requiring time commitment, vulnerability and the threat of rejection. Transfer growth, on the other hand, is easy. Church-hoppers are not afraid; they will eat out of your hand, and they often love being stolen.

This shift in the evangelistic focus of the church has been noted before,[33] but the depth of the problem has never been fully established. Not only have the church growth movement and the evangelical church developed a taste for transfer growth, but they have retooled church programming to specialize in it.

One of the most popular "evangelistic outreach" programs for U.S. churches is vacation Bible school. Over the past few years churches have spent hundreds of thousands of dollars nationwide to present the popular Veggie Tales VBS program. In our city I saw at least a half a dozen church lawns with signs announcing the dates and times of the VBS program.

But if we are honest, I expect your church experience is like ours. The kids who come are the kids who are in the church. Now we have ways to improve the evangelistic mix of our crowd, but normally we attract the already churched.

It is not surprising because we are advertising to Christians. First of all, who has ever heard of Veggie Tales except people in the Christian subculture? Bob the Tomato and Larry the Cucumber are a Christian thing. Second, in our information-soaked postmodern society, how much impact does a sign on a church lawn have? Third, even if a secular parent sees the sign, knows who the vegetables are and does not hate churches, it is highly unlikely that in this day and age they will drop off their daughter to spend several hours in a big building with total strangers. The only people who will fall for that setup are Christians! Like it or not, our hottest evangelistic outreach for the summer is geared to the already churched.

Yet that target market could be changed in a heartbeat. Take the very same program and hold it in a backyard in a neighborhood where the church members live, and the secular neighbors will bring their kids over every time. We have done this on many occasions with tremendous response and have seen lives surrendered to God. But we have to think outside of the church box.

Christian radio is another way we preach to the choir. I am on the board of WMSJ-FM, the only Christian contemporary radio station in northern New England. We cater to an exclusively Christian audience of twenty-five thousand people. We play only Christian music; our news broadcast and editorials take a Christian perspective, and we air a host of Christian program personalities.

Why on earth does the station receive call after call from churches wanting it to develop a "hot," "exciting," "alluring" radio spot that hawks their church programs and service times? Our audience is the churched!

Mark, the station manager, often tries to dissuade them and encourages them to list their service instead on a secular station. Now *there* is a spot for a church ad. This suggestion was so often met with displeasure that we have had to formulate an explicit policy: a church's ad must include the phrase "if you are new to our community and looking for a church home." It is our way of saying that church hopping is not supported here.

What about the intention of Sunday-evening services? Perhaps there was a day when evangelistic services on Sunday night were the norm, but I think the actual activity of Sunday evenings nowadays is church shopping. Many times after a seminar or class I have been approached by someone who exclaims, "Pastor, I liked your talk. Do you have an evening service? I think I'd like to bring my wife over and try you out."

Still attending their home church and not wanting their wanderlust to be public information, many church hoppers try out churches on Sunday nights. And what does the church do in response? We desperately seek to attract them with concerts, special events and seminars, complete with good follow-up to assimilate these new arrivals into our fellowship. Sunday evenings for church hoppers has become the QVC channel where they can examine the wares of a church before they make their move.

Even the church's last vestige of the great revivals, itinerant preaching, has gone domestic. Walking up the steps of the Civic Center, I was amazed to see an open-air evangelist shouting at passersby at the top of his lungs. King James Bible clutched firmly, waving tracts with his church's address and service times stamped on the back, he earnestly and dynamically proclaimed his message.

What surprised me was that my wife and I had arrived to attend a Wayne Watson concert. The preacher was preaching to Christians. To Carol's utter chagrin, I gave in to an impulse to make sure he knew.

"Do you know why all these people are here tonight?" I asked.

"Yes, for the Wayne Watson concert," he replied.

"Do you know that they are probably all Christians?"

"Yes, I suppose that's true."

"Well then, what are you doing?"

"I'm evangelizing. I'm starting a new church on Broadway, and

I'm out here to preach and share these tracts. Want one?"

Unbelievably, transfer growth has effectively replaced the lost with the found as our target market! Consuming our tithes and our time, this inverted inreach has become the dark side's crowning achievement. Satan has successfully refocused the church—and his tool is growth for growth's sake. Pure numerical increase has become our first love.

John Stott reflects on a warning issued in the book of Revelation: " 'But I have this against you, that you have abandoned the love you first had.' They had left their first love. They had fallen from the early heights of devotion to Christ, which they had climbed. They had descended to the plains of mediocrity."[34] Just so we have, I am afraid, lowered our standards. Our mission has been compromised and our goals errantly framed.

A Weak Foundation

The seventh and final deadly sin: a weak foundation. Jesus warns that a house built outside of his teachings—that is, built on worldly principles—is a house built on sand. "The rain came down, the streams rose, and the winds blew and beat against that house, and it fell with a great crash" (Mt 7:27).

Transfer growth is weak growth. The people who leave one church for another often arrive at their new home with lots of emotional and spiritual baggage.

That baggage frequently places demands on the ministry that will shift its vision. Emotional and spiritual baggage consumes both the owner of the luggage and those who seek to assist in carrying it. Beware of the demands—counseling, personnel resources, finances and time. It only takes a few wounded people to keep a full-time pastor very tied up.

Transfer growth is also very uncommitted growth. Church hopping is a manifestation of some inability to become part of a body. Rarely does that issue resolve itself. Unless the hurt is healed or the motivation discovered, confronted and brought to resolution, transferees will probably run headlong into the same problem in your church. Trying to build a house on shifting members is a confusing and fruitless endeavor.

The same holds true for those who have confused a need for spiritual growth with a need to change churches. How many times have people told me that they were not being fed in their old church? For that matter, how many people have left *my* ministry because they were not being fed?

Some labor under the misconception that churches are fixed and limited in their ability to offer opportunities for growth. Nothing could be further from the truth. Churches are living organisms. With the power of the Holy Spirit, they mature and develop depth and character over time.

It is profoundly arrogant to assume that you are the one person in the kingdom of God whom Jesus has selected to be on some sort of spiritual fast track, so that you need to consume every church in the tristate region to support your incredible growth. Quite the contrary: such an ignorance of what really matters, such a lack of love, betrays not spiritual depth but shallowness.

One of the richer aspects of my spiritual growth was learning the value of little things—a child's embrace, the structure of my hand, one attribute of God. The more you focus, the more you notice what you had not seen before. The body of Christ is like that. You can spend a lifetime growing in one place if you are willing to yield your wisdom in favor of his.

Weak growth is built on bad habits. Sheep that have been running the range never will be content in a fold again. What transferred into your church will surely transfer out of your church.

The best way I know to build a church is through the honest labor of conversion growth. People who came to faith through your investment in their lives will never forget your faithfulness and love. In a church, that translates into dedicated workers for the Lord and sweet friendships for the pastor. If you want a strong foundation, rekindle the fires of revival in your messages and take every opportunity the Lord affords you to lead another to Christ.

Rick Warren points to the importance of building a church on a solid foundation:

> The foundation determines both size and the strength of a building. You can never build larger than the foundation can handle. The same is true for churches. A church built on an inadequate or faulty foundation will never reach the height that God intends for it to reach. It will topple over once it outgrows its base.[35]

Conclusion

This chapter has exposed the cost—seven deadly sins—that transfer growth has extracted from the church. Now it is time to begin to develop guidelines that will stop transfer growth from running rampant in our congregations and help bring healing and wholeness back to the church.

6

The Good Shepherd

He tends his flock like a shepherd:
He gathers the lambs in his arms
and carries them close to his heart;
he gently leads. ISAIAH 40:11

We were six hundred feet up the face of White Horse Cliff in New Hampshire's White Mountains. Nightfall was upon us, and we still had over four hundred feet of vertical climb to go. Four of us were standing on a piece of ledge scarcely the size of a shoe. It was late October, and the temperature was dropping. Water was seeping out of the crack we were trying to climb, making ascent impossible. The situation was grave.

"Well, we need to make a commitment move." Ollie, our lead climber, understood that we could not survive the night on the face of the cliff. There was a handhold just out of reach that held promise of a path to the top. But the only way to grab it was to commit your full body momentum toward it, forever giving up the security of the little ledge. We could climb no higher, and we could not survive the night where we were, yet to commit ourselves to an unseen and untested handhold required God-given faith and discipline.

Changing the way we deal with transfer growth will require a commitment move. Leaving the safety of growth that trickles in year by year for a new position that will not permit stealing sheep can feel very threatening. Yet for the church to remain where it is, stuck on the ledge of no kingdom growth, would allow a slow death of hypothermia to claim its life.

In rock climbing we call this point the sharp end of the rope. The first climber needs to find the path to the top. Unsecured by belay lines, he faces the challenge of picking the right route and securing protection in the rock wall for those who follow.

This chapter is about the sharp end of the rope. A few churches and pastors have already committed themselves to the position of not embracing transfer growth. Their stories are told here, for they offer us protection: they have succeeded in moving from being a church that steals for its existence to being a church that harvests its own crops.

There are several areas in the life of the church that will have to drastically change if we are to overcome the powerful allurement of transfer growth. First, we must develop an evangelistic focus that is effective in reaching the lost for Christ. Second, we must explore ways to develop covenants with other area churches to help sustain a "no transfer growth" policy. Third, we must change the standard way we respond to church hopping and related issues. Fourth, we need to define times when transfer growth *is* good shepherding.

The Problem with Lift

There has been a subtle shift over the years toward the *lifting* of the evangelical community and the church. Lift, a phenomenon studied in missiology, occurs in cultures that are exposed to the teachings of Jesus Christ. As the cultures embrace Christianity, they discover that obeying God's laws leads to increased prosperity.

When the sluggard goes to work, when the thief ceases to steal and when people honor God with their tithes, the Lord's blessing is bestowed on the people.

The result of lift is a changing of people's lifestyle. The once naked native now can be found in shirt and a tie. Multiple wives are replaced with one spouse. The literacy rate rises: due to a desire to read God's Word, education is promoted. Lift places the evangelized population in a better economic and social bracket.

In cultures where the gospel is more established, lift might be seen as the transformation from a hungry little fellowship meeting in the basement of someone's house to an established worship center on a prime piece of property. Such a transition, usually the product of earnest evangelistic outreach, brings several changes in the church that affect evangelism.

Middle Age

First, middle-age values and expectations creep in. Resources come to be invested more on sustaining the church's comfort zone than on growing the church. Buildings are bought, multiple staff hired, and programming, lots of programming, is created to meet the needs of members of a better-educated and wealthier social stratum.

In the process of aging the cutting edge of the evangelical movement becomes dulled. Once highly evangelistic church plants like the Vineyard and Calvary Chapel have become static institutions. Gone are the lean years when conversion growth was the center of the church's focus; now we are in the fat years of protecting our own interests.

Too severe? Several years ago I was looking at my church's budget for the year, because I have come to realize that our budget expresses our real actions in ministry. It dawned on me that we were spending a very small percent of our money on true evangelistic outreach. We had become fat. In our middle age we were spending the lion's share of our budget on ourselves. Lift was setting in.

Convicted, I stood before our church and told of my discovery. We are a small church, so much of our budget sustains operating costs, but what about the need to be doing the work of an evangelist? We claimed to be an evangelical church, but we were not investing in the harvest. That day we pledged to change, to cease being ruled by self-interest. We decided to get rid of our paunchy midsection and developed an aggressive exercise program of giving till it hurt.

We offered valuable office space to evangelistic parachurch organizations. At first they did not trust us. The church wants to do what? But after a time Young Life moved in, Wellspring Counseling moved in, Exodus International moved in, each finding a home base for its operations. Empowering these Christ-beckoning ministries to succeed made us feel positive about our outreach. But it was not enough.

Our missions program had been good. We tithed our income and held weekend missions conferences once a year, but our involvement in missions was sterile. We were sitting on the couch flicking the remote, experiencing missions vicariously and losing our evangelistic muscle tone. We needed some exercise.

In the past several years our small church has logged over sixty-one thousand person-hours on foreign soil sharing the gospel of Jesus Christ. Last Sunday the congregation commissioned its first missionary in over one hundred years! Nicole had been called into world missions as she went on our mission trips as a teenager. Exercise was bringing renewed health to the clogged arteries of our heart for evangelism. But we did not stop there; the program was starting to feel good, so we pressed on.

Eighty percent of all conversion growth comes from individuals below the age of eighteen. How could we call ourselves evangelical and ignore this part of the harvest? In an attempt do Christ-honoring work with this prime "target market," we hyper-extended our budget and hired a full-time youth pastor. Then we gave him away to Young Life as a paid full-time staff person to reach high-schoolers. Our kids are taken care of by lay leaders in the church; we wanted to be working in the harvest.

I am embarrassed to say that the result of all this giving has been nothing but problems. Cars are crowding the curbs on the street, kids are packing out the Sunday school space, and there is standing room only for the worship service.

As conservative as I am, I cannot help but be enthusiastic about God's pleasure with the commitment moves we made to focus on conversion growth. With a twinkle in his eye, J. Christy Wilson always used to say that if you want your church to grow, honor Christ in your giving to evangelization.

Combating the effects of lift means that you have to make some radical changes. It is not easy to rechannel and refocus a church's goals and objectives. Middle age is the power curve of life, when enjoying the fruit of our labor is a constant temptation. But we should not take lightly these words spoken by Christ:

> "You still lack one thing. Sell everything you have and give to the poor, and you will have treasure in heaven. Then come, follow me."
> When [the young man] heard this, he became very sad, because he was a man of great wealth. Jesus looked at him and said, "How hard it is for the rich to enter the kingdom of God! Indeed, it is easier for a camel to go through the eye of a needle than for a rich man to enter the kingdom of God." (Lk 18:22-25)

God gave your church its talent as an investment to be used for the kingdom. So spend the money. The church needs to grow lean again, placing its faith not on endowment funds but on the Lord. It can then rekindle the fires of evangelism and refocus its energies on conversion growth.

Lift Attracts Lift

Lift in a church works to refocus its growth. Lift attracts lift. In this fashion, churches begin the process of developing contacts and building relational bridges to people who are "just like us." This homogeneous group factor often tends to move the church out of two of the most target-rich environments for evangelism.

First, the lost. Lift places people in a stratum of spiritual comfort and knowledge that is alien to the culture. Jesus predicted that his words would created division (Lk 12:49), and that the message and the messengers would be rejected (Jn 15:18—16:4). Most of us by nature do not enjoy conflict or rejection. It is easier not only to relate to our natural biological webs of influence (Ralph Winter's theory) but also to our spiritual webs of influence. In this manner lift draws us away from the lost and causes us to travel predominately in circles where we derive companionship from spiritually like-minded people.

The effect of this process, as will be discussed further in this chapter, is the domestication of our evangelistic zeal. We find ourselves inviting the already churched to our services, and gradually we all but abandon the lost. This, I dare to contend, has adversely affected the conversion growth effectiveness of the church, contributing, perhaps significantly, to the decline in evangelical populations over the past several decades.

In the same fashion, our sense of obligation to the lost becomes replaced with a selfish sense of comfort. This is the "middle age" effect of lift as it creates spiritual prosperity. We actually develop a lower tolerance for the unchurched person's ignorance and faux pas regarding the accepted norms of the church subculture. Frankly, we can develop a list of attributes that have caused the seeker to dub Christians as snobs. We can tend to be arrogant, haughty, boastful, proud and rude, creating an elite society through this process of lift.

Debbie, a single mom with two little girls, came to church one Sunday because her husband had left them, and she was seeking God. She knew some of the people in our church and came because of the support they had shown her. She was shy and nervous, and she seemed to feel out of place. She did not have a Bible, nor did she wear a dress, and the words to the songs were obviously foreign to her.

Then it happened—an ecclesiastical/social faux pas. One of her little girls began fussing. In spite of Debbie's best efforts, the traditional polite silence of sermon time proved too long a period of restriction for this little girl. Fussing turned into audible defiance. Debbie did not know what to do, so in a panic-induced moment she grabbed the little girl by the scruff of the neck and hauled her out the doors of the sanctuary into the foyer. Sadly, Debbie returned to collect her other daughter and was never seen in our church again.

The story did not end there. Years later, quite by accident, I stumbled onto what Paul Harvey would say was the rest of the story. When Debbie entered the foyer, unbeknownst to me, she had been accosted by an older woman who obviously felt that Debbie should have known better than to bring children into the sanctuary. She was asked why her husband was not helping her control her children. Then she was told a lie! "Our pastor does not like children or noise in the church service. Leave your daughters in our junior church area, or leave them home."

Lift can disassociate us from a dying world. We have attractive carpets, nicely arranged bulletins, cleanly painted walls and deep subculture norms. The unchurched do not fit in to this world. When the middle age of lift sets in, churched people can become upset with the headaches of having newborns in the house; we are past that stage of life. We desire to plan our retirement and find ways of increasing our spiritual and physical comfort levels. The "not like us" gain the disfavor of an unwanted pregnancy and can, in many subtle ways, be aborted.

To combat these tendencies a church needs to make a conscious commitment to be sensitive toward individuals who have not yet discovered a relationship with Jesus Christ. Commonly identified in church growth circles as being seeker sensitive, this process breaks the unconscious cycle of lift as churches focus on providing welcoming, safe environments for the lost.

This conscious commitment needs to occur on several different levels. First, it must be the passion and conviction of the *church*

leadership. To attain this unity requires some hard work. Rick Warren, in his book *The Purpose-Driven Church,* identifies that a
church's starting point for effective ministry that reaches outward is
found through identifying its purpose. "If you want to build a
healthy, strong, and growing church you must spend time laying a
solid foundation. This is done by clarifying in the minds of everyone involved exactly why the church exists and what it is supposed to do. There is incredible power in having a clearly defined
purpose statement."[1]

This process begins in the Word of God. When we encounter
God's plan for his church in the Scriptures, it defines for us our
mission in the world. Many of the successful church growth pastors I have known have either written or commented on one exercise they undertook that changed the hearts of their churches.
They spent time in Bible study and discovery with their leadership
with the expressed purpose of defining the purpose of their
church.[2]

Many pastors never begin at this basic starting point. Leadership
meetings are times of expediting the urgent and focusing on the
problems in the ministry. This serves only to perpetuate the ignorance that empowers the ill effects of lift. Creating a spiritual component to the leadership's life, especially one that helps them to
define their philosophy of ministry, is invaluable.

Defining the church's purpose needs to be captured in a missional statement that constantly serves as a touchstone, focusing
the church on its primary goals. The statement needs to be biblical,
specific, transferable and measurable. By *biblical* I mean that a
church's primary objectives should reflect the objectives of God.
Specific means it is clear. *Transferable* expresses the need for the
statement to be easily assimilated by people, and *measurable* indicates the ability to tell whether or not an objective is on task by
looking at the mission statement.

"To know Christ and to make him known" is the missional statement of Saint Paul's Church in Darien, Connecticut—Christ-cen-

tered, definitive, catchy and very orienting. This statement defines the core elements of this church's mission as desiring to grow in faith in Christ and being evangelically oriented in their mission. This is an excellent example of what you want to produce.

Mission statements help to protect a church from becoming lift oriented. They provide a sense of direction and a sounding board for decision-making processes.

Several years ago our church built an addition. It was a modest endeavor, but for us the new annex quickly became a source of accomplishment and pride. Shortly after it was completed the carpets began to retain staining from the children utilizing the annex as a pathway to their Sunday school rooms.

When our church leadership met, this issue was brought up. Initially the conversation in the room centered around finding ways to keep the children out of the new annex. Suddenly it dawned on us that this was ridiculous. Our mission statement includes the words "to make Christ known." The purpose of this new annex was not so that we could increase our comfort level by enjoying pristine carpets. We built it so that we could reach these kids for Christ. What were we doing locking its doors?

That night we decided that if our carpets needed to be replaced every few years (and they do), then that was faithful stewardship. Our leadership experienced a paradigm shift, one that moved us off the self-centered focuses of lift and on to becoming a place that created a genuinely warm environment for seekers.

Second, the *church body* needs to be trained in knowing both what the church's mission statement is and what it means to do it.

It simply is not enough for a church to develop a neat mission statement and for the leadership to like it. This statement needs to become a central component in the heart and soul of the church. Every member of the church should be able to state this statement because every member of the church will need to know the church's mission so that they can discern if they are in fact a piece of the process of attaining that goal.

For some churches this will occur as a result of engaging their congregation in the process of developing a mission statement. Free Christian Church of Andover, Massachusetts, undertook the task of developing a mission statement that reflected the passions and Christward thoughts of their people. Pastor Jack Daniel took great pains to survey, refine and produce a statement that captured the heart and hopes of their church. In this process, the church gained intimate ownership.

Other churches will have boards or special committees develop this statement. Such was the case in our church. At Stroudwater the primary place where we "transfer" our mission statement to our congregation is in our corporate worship environment. Here, at the start of our worship service our mission statement is shared every Sunday. This has become an effective tool both in unifying the body by proclaiming our purpose and in celebrating our covenant together before the Lord.

The aspects of your mission statement can also be regularly emphasized in your sermons. When preaching expositorially, do not pass lightly over a text that touches on your church's purpose. Chew on the passage, like a dog worrying a bone, and create tangible applications. If your preference is topical preaching, develop a series that helps your church understand the biblical principles behind your mission statement, and teach them how to act on those principles in their world.

It is appropriate to have your mission statement printed on your church letterhead, business cards and other publications that your congregation may see. You can also use these "slogans" to help outsiders learn something about your church. Placing your mission statement on your church sign or under your listing in the yellow pages serves as a simple way to give seekers a taste of what it is your church is about.

Taking this simple step will help your church safeguard itself from the effects of spiritual lift. We must forever remember that at one time in our pilgrimage toward Christ, someone accepted us in spite of our spiritual ignorance and invested in the task of bringing us to faith. I believe that the apostle Paul addresses the subject of spiritual lift when he wrote the church in Rome: "Do not think of yourself more highly than you ought, but rather think of yourself with sober judgment, in accordance with the measure of faith God has given you" (Rom 12:3).

Economic Lift

Second, lift creates economic prosperity. This has a tendency to move Christians into the upper levels of whatever social stratum it is that they are in. This effect actually has a bearing on evangelism. It begins to move Christians away from that group of people who historically have always been the most receptive to the gospel, *the poor.*

Dr. Richard Lovelace once pointed out in a lecture that almost all the revivals in history began in the lower economic stratum of society. Jesus certainly experienced greater success with the common masses then he did among the social elite. John Wesley's outreach with the coal miners in England is another example of this trend, as are the recent revivals in Latin America.

When lift helps a Christian leave poverty there understandably appears to be little interest in returning for that person. This has been a problem in the mission field. Seeking to create national leaders, evangelists and pastors for third world countries, many missions organizations have in the past selected promising students from these countries and sent them to the United States or Europe for training. Upon graduation we have discovered that many of these students, once they have enjoyed economic prosperity abroad, do not want to return to their native land.

Lift locates churches on the other side of the tracks, causes the people to dress differently and changes the types of folks with which they want to associate. In this manner the poor, one of the highest evangelistic success strata in the world, are commonly forgotten.

How can we correct this trend? Obviously by reinvesting our

time, talents and tithes back into this harvest field. There are practical steps to take, but to act on them requires us to be at a common commitment level for the task at hand. That level is best acquired by understanding what it is that God expects of wealthy churches and what it means to love even the poor deeply from our hearts.

Economic Koinonia

Ronald Sider, in his book *Rich Christians in an Age of Hunger,* outlines a helpful guideline for giving that the apostle Paul developed for the church at Corinth. Sider's primary interest was in involving the church in the fight against world hunger, but the principles speak also to the fight against spiritual hunger experienced by the poor.

> Paul's first guideline for sharing in the body of believers was general: *Give all you can.* Each person should give "as he may prosper" (1 Cor. 16:2). But that does not mean a small donation that costs nothing. Paul praised the Macedonians who "gave according to their means . . . and beyond their means" (2 Cor. 8:3).[3]

To fight economic lift, churches that experience prosperity need to give generously to the impoverished works of God that need financial support.

Pastor Phil Strout of the Greater Portland Vineyard Christian Fellowship gave an excellent example of this type of support. "We had heard about an ethnic inner city church in Portland that could not meet a financial need they had. This church works with minority immigrants who settle in our city. So our elders met and decided to send this church a check to cover this expense. It was for several thousand dollars, and the gift both blessed their ministry and blessed our congregation. We felt *good* about investing in the work they were doing for the kingdom."

What impressed me was not the fact that Phil's church gave that money. I was impressed that they were so generous at a time when their church was heavily engaged in a fundraising campaign to acquire a badly needed new facility. They gave from the muscle of their finances, and not from the fat of their surpluses. This type of giving directly counterattacks the self-indulging tendencies that churches often experience as a result of economic lift.

Sider's second Pauline guideline is "to remember that giving is voluntary (2 Cor. 8:3). Paul specifically noted that he was not issuing a command to the Corinthians (2 Cor. 8:8). Legalism is not the answer."[4]

In some cases where mandatory giving is required, churches and individuals simply submit lump sums to their denominations, allowing the mother institution to invest all of their resources. I think that is unfortunate. It is too sterile and removes your church from the act of engaging in the life of a ministry. This causes our giving to become conservative and obligatory instead of the bold radical type of giving that the New Testament church enjoyed (Acts 2:44).

People are far more generous with their resources when they are empowered to be good stewards of their resources. That simply means they like to know who, what, when, where and how their gift is going to be invested. Rick Warren has stated in his church stewardship seminars that "people have many pockets. Informing them and offering multiple opportunities for participation increases the giving levels of the people in your church."

One Sunday morning I witnessed the truth of this concept. A friend of mine from Sierra Leone, West Africa, was visiting my family in New Hampshire. During the sharing time in our church, Samuel stood up and told of his work among his people. He quite innocently expressed a need for a bicycle to aid him in his ministerial travel. Moved by the Spirit our elders decided to take a second offering for this brother. I was amazed to see a small congregation that already was strongly supporting their church pony up an additional five hundred dollars on the spot for this brother.

People like to give to ministries they know. As wealthy churches that means that we should engage in partnerships with churches who are working with the poor, because it will inspire us to be boldly generous with our resources. In some cases that may mean adopting a sister church on the mission field in a Third World country or sharing your wealth with the churches in need in your community.

The last of Paul's guidelines offered by Sider is what he calls "the most startling." "The norm, he [Paul] suggests, is something like economic equality among the people of God. 'I do not mean that others should be eased and you burdened, but that as a matter of equality your abundance at the present time should supply their want, so that their abundance may supply your want, that there may be equality.' To support his principle, Paul quotes from the biblical story of the manna. 'As it is written, "he who gathered much had nothing left over, and he who gathered little had no lack"' (2 Cor. 8:13-15)."[5]

Giving our abundance is not always about doling out cash. Sometimes we can give to the poor through the sharing of our resources. This is especially true for churches regarding the issue of facilities. Many church facilities stand unused for six out of seven days. That represents an abundance of time that could be transformed into an effective gift to another for the purpose of reaching the poor.

Pastor Art Gay and the First Baptist Church of Portland are a classic case of a church that is combating economic lift by sharing the abundance of their resources. On Sundays, once their worship service is over, First Baptist does not just close their doors. Instead, they share their sanctuary and classroom space with other churches in our community who cannot afford to purchase their own facility. In this fashion Pastor Gay's church has encouraged a Russian church, an African church and an Asian church. These ministries work with refugees who come to our city seeking the safety that America offers. Empowered by First Baptist, they are able to reach crosscultural minority groups within the very borders of our home state of Maine.

Direct involvement with the poor is a point I deliberately saved for last. Most churches are well intending in regard to this point, but few have the long-term commitment to work with the troubled and impoverished people in their geographic areas. I have seen churches inspired by a special message or motivated by guilt attempt to reach out to the poor, and in the end, experience the overwhelming futility of failing to meet needs. Discouraged, they suffer the double indemnity of demoralizing their body and deserting the impoverished whom they had attempted to serve.

Let me affirm those churches that feel called to work significantly with the impoverished. I personally spent years as a part of a Salvation Army ministry that reached out to the street people, prostitutes and pimps of Boston's inner city. But let me also warn that this level of ministry demands much from your church's resources.

For churches experiencing economic lift, I would recommend another option to the traditional soup kitchens or street evangelistic efforts. Discover ministries or people who are working effectively with the poor and partner with them. You do not have to reinvent the wheel, and your energies and resources can greatly empower those who are committed and gifted to work in this harvest field.

Munjoy Hill represents the tough end of Portland. Federal housing units attract families who clearly are the poor of our city. In the middle of this community Dale Carlson planted the Root Cellar. From humble beginnings the Root Cellar has expanded to be one of the most effective urban ministries in New England.

Part of the Root Cellar's success has been not just in helping the poor, but in helping the suburban churches to partner in this experience. Carlson and his excellent staff pour hundreds of hours into developing relationships with area churches, allowing the members of these churches to go and minister to the poor (hands on) in safe and long-term environments.[6] In this fashion, church members fulfill their need to be in touch with the ministry, and churches can give financial and physical support to evangelizing an often overlooked financial stratum.

Low Tolerance Diet

In our fight against the middle-age bulge produced by life, we must get back in shape by changing our diet. We need to stop eating junk food. Cheap growth, transfer growth, fills the building without adding muscle to the body. The message of no tolerance for church hopping needs to be established in the church, beginning on Sunday morning. The message "We are not interested in transfer growth" needs to be clearly expressed in a variety of ways.

First, the greeting. When opening comments are addressed to the attendees, you can acknowledge visitors, thank them for coming, and ask them to take your church's greeting back to their home church next week. Immediately you have acknowledged their church and shown a sign of love and solidarity with that fellowship.

During the prayer time, pray for other pastors and churches of your community. Pray for them by name, and mention one positive thing about them in the prayer. Thank God for their unity with your church and for their hard work in the harvest. Honor them and express love for them. This demonstrates the high value you place on their ministry and creates an awkward atmosphere for a potential church hopper.

Third, during the offering do not take visitors' money. This may sound crazy, but inform your visitors that they are your guests and that it is the members of the church who will pay for the ministry of the church. Any visiting unbelievers will be impressed; you have gained some hard-earned integrity.

Follow up this statement up with another: "If you are visiting us from another church today, please be sure to place your tithe in your church's offering when you return home next week." The church hopper is confronted, and their financial means of influence is unplugged.

Finally, if you greet people at the door after the service and are introduced to someone who is visiting from an area church, immediately and positively acknowledge their pastor. If you know the pastor personally, make mention of your last time together; if not, express your delight with that pastor's work. People leaving a church under the wrong conditions become very uncomfortable when it appears that another pastor supports theirs. If the folks begin speaking negatively about their pastor's ministry, quickly encourage them to seek out the pastor and talk it over.

Whenever I have practiced these principles, persons who were considering a church change seem to have returned to their home church. But what happens if they still attend your church? Have "the talk." Some churches have pastoral or lay leader visitation programs designed to assimilate visitors into the church. The church growth movement is big on initial contact, having found that 82 percent of all first-time visitors who are contacted within twenty-four hours return. That is an impressive statistic.

At this point we need to be very honest with people. It is not always easy. I have had some angry and hurt responses from folks who viewed their move to our church as a blessing for them and us. So ingrained is the perceived right to church hop that to confront it is often deemed offensive.

Drawing the line in the sand forces people to confront their issues. It promotes health and protects your church from developing a weak foundation. Your seats are saved for the lost, and you will have time to focus on them.

Covenants of Care

Why has real unity been elusive for the church? Perhaps the fear of losing people from our churches prompts us to lay great emphasis on our theological distinctives. We have to find some error in our brother or sister to discourage our flock from wandering. So we wage holy wars on each other. This is a foolish and unwarranted enterprise that distracts us from our real adversary, the devil. Who is watching out for his fiery darts when churches are engaged in

drive-by shootings? As my best friend's mom said when I accidentally hit my head with a hammer, "You've smacked your silly own
self."

During World War II the Allied forces endured months of prolonged fighting not caused by brilliant enemy tactics but by jealous
infighting. The British, French and American armies had abandoned planned battle strategies to gain glory and the accolades of
the people by vying to be the first to liberate important European
cities.

Each jeopardized the mission as the enemy took advantage of
the aborted sections of the offensive lines. Thousands of troops
died and months were added to the conflict because of the self-
centered displays of immaturity. As long as a united front remains
elusive for the church, we suffer similar devastating losses.

"So what are you going to do about this?" Pastor Bob Freder-
ichs, of the Vision New England Pastoral Mentoring program was
doing what he does best, holding me accountable. Once I had
articulated my convictions regarding transfer growth, he wanted to
know how I was going to spread the word to the other churches in
our city. "You know, Bill," he not so gently prodded, "this is
important information. You need to share your convictions in the
Evangelical Pastors' Fellowship."

What a great place to start. Early critics of my thesis on stealing
sheep had pointed to what they saw as my unrealistic hope that
churches could band together to promote non-transfer growth policies in cities or regions. "It may work in Maine," wrote one critic,
"but how will it work in L.A., or Dallas?"

The answer lies in using networks of influence that have
already been established in your area. Most regions now have
some kind of pastors' fellowship. Many evangelical pastors meet
regularly for prayer and enjoy other forms of fellowship. If such
groups agreed to promote non-transfer growth policies, a very
positive and unifying bond could be achieved.

Is this unrealistic? In Hopkinton, Massachusetts, such a model of unity exists. Pastor Dick Germaine told me, "When I started ministering here in Hopkinton our church experienced substantial growth. Then I began to realize the very thing that you are talking about. We were seeing a lot of people simply transferring in from other churches."

The wrongness of this struck Pastor Germaine, and he began to develop new standards for growth in his church. "We addressed the issue of church transfers. It was not how we wanted to grow, so we discouraged the practice."

In actuality Germaine went well beyond discouraging the practice. He formed a "Covenant of Pastoral Integrity" between his church and the other churches in his area. "They are wonderful people," said Germaine. "The purpose of this covenant was to protect each other's ministries and promote healthy relationships in the church community."

Today Hopkinton, located just north of Boston, has a network of seventeen churches that affirm a non-transfer growth policy. Their covenant follows—an effective model for bringing an end to the damaging effects of sheep stealing.

Covenant of Pastoral Integrity

When we become aware that a person or family from one of our churches visits more than one time the church of another of us, the pastor of the church being visited will notify the pastor of the church the person or family is from. The pastor of the home church, or a representative chosen by him, will either call or visit the person or family to see if all is well.

If the person or family continues to visit the new church, the pastor of the new church will call or visit the person or family to determine why they are coming, and try to help resolve any problem or sense of alienation, etc. the person or family has with their home church, pastor, people, etc. The pastor of the new church will challenge the person or family from scripture to work out the relational problem or problems with the home church and to be reconciled. The pastor of the new church may possibly be able to fill the role of a mediator between the person or family and the person or persons who are part of the problem. He should attempt to arrange a meeting with the involved parties (1 Peter 3:11).

The pastor of the church being visited will keep the pastor of the home church informed of what is happening with the person or family.

If the person or family visiting the new church is living in sin and not repenting, the pastor of the new church will refuse that person or family membership in their church until repentance has been experienced. If they are not seeking membership but keep coming, the pastor of the new church will meet with the new people/person and attempt to help them deal with why they are leaving their own church.

We will need to recognize that there are times when a person or family needs a change of church because of inner needs or family needs. We will need to be supportive of such people at such times.

For the sake of the kingdom of God, the church must seek this type of unified front. I applaud this wonderful example of mutual respect and love and am humbled by the tremendous effort these men and women are making to bring harmony to the body of Christ.

For the adverse affects of transfer growth to effectively be ended, we need to grow in love. Churches in each region and each city need to begin the process of supporting and embracing one another. Overcoming doctrinal differences and embracing the orthodox tenets of our faith are necessary in an age that challenges the very core of the church's validity.

Steve Macchia and his team have done a brilliant service to the churches in New England through the skillful development of Vision New England. This is an interdenominational resource center that seeks to promote health between the members of the body of Christ through equipping and training. Not only is training in specific areas of ministry a priority, but fellowship is as well.

Each February over ten thousand Christians assemble in Boston for an event called Congress—three days of worship, teaching and fellowship. It is the only ministry of its kind in the United States. Its emphasis on community is bridging gaps between many of New England's churches. "The thrill of singing with thousands of brothers and sisters in Christ," said one participant in the event, "makes me want to be with them forever." Well, that's good news!

Transfer Growth at the Top

To turn the tide of transfer growth we need to establish a different model of commitment at the top. Churches in our throw-away society, with disposable everything, have grown much too used to short-term pastoral engagements. In a lecture on church growth C. Peter Wagner noted, "The average length of time that a senior pastor stays in a church is two years, and the average youth pastor's tenure is seven months."

Pastors are perhaps the most egregious church hoppers. In seminary many young students learn to expect to lose their first charge due to either blunders that require their hasty retreat or, if they are good at what they do, a better offer. Being stolen is what delineates the arc of a pastor's career. Bigger churches issue calls, and we entertain the option of church hopping. No wonder parishioners learn to do it!

The best preacher I ever heard shattered this traditional model of pastoral church hopping for me. He was my Hebrew professor in seminary and pastored a small congregation of forty very plain people in a New England fishing village.

As the chaplain of the seminary, I had heard the best speakers in the world in our chapels, and this man's preaching was second to none. Puzzled by his dedication to this small church I confronted him one Sunday: "What are you doing here? You are the best teacher I have ever had; you are the best preacher I have ever heard; you graduated magna cum laude from Harvard. You could be the pastor of the church of your choice."

His answer was filled with wisdom and insight: "God loves these people, and they deserve my best to show them God's faithfulness." Indeed they did, and suddenly I began to see that if ministry is to blossom, relationships and trust must be developed through faithfulness.

According to Carl George, "Long term pastorates are the most productive ministries in the world today. There is a direct correlation between church size and health, and the stability of the pastoral staff."[7]

Pastoral ministry is about investing. When I came to this, my second church, I challenged the search committee. I asked that if they called me, they consider it a call for life. For my end of this bargain, I promised to keep on growing in the Lord and not lapse into a monotonous ministry. For their part of the relationship, they would facilitate my growth by underwriting my continuing education and they would promise to grow with me. It was a commitment to build relationships and provide a safe place to grow so that we could experience real community.

Long-term investments in people's lives and walks produce a stable and deep relationship between the pastor and the congregation. Differences are worked on with a much higher degree of integrity, because we are all going to be staying together for a very long time.

In such an environment, failure is not terminal; it is readily viewed as a part of the corporate pilgrimage. This model kills transfer growth and shines the light of Christ in a culture where such commitment is all too rare.

Pastoral Love

One of the most powerful, practical tools to combat transfer growth is small group ministry. In small groups people form the bonds of love that hold the community together. It is in this environment that I can fulfill my ministry vision, "to help people fall passionately in love with Jesus Christ."

All too often I have seen a lack of pastoral commitment to facilitating community through small groups. It is not enough that your church has small groups; you need to be involved in one, experiencing the joy of sharing your life in Christ with your parishioners. My wife, Carol, and I have learned the value of this experience.

For the past ten years we have hosted small group meetings in our home. Each year, we form a new group of twelve people who commit to being together for a one-year block of time. In these groups we worship, study, pray and develop deep relational bonds. Over the course of these ten years, we have grown to personally know 120 of our parishioners. This has created a rich and healthy environment of love and understanding between our call to ministry and our church.

Rescuing the Churched Lost

Pastor Phil roared with laughter when I asked his thoughts about the possibility of healthy transfer growth. "Oh," he exclaimed, "isn't that when I trade you two of my Jezebels for one of your Judases?"

Healthy transfer growth is about rescuing sheep. In some cases they are rescued from a church where salvation is not articulated. In other cases they are rescued from a setting where false teaching and heresy occur. And some sheep need to be rescued from abusive church settings.

By definition, the "churched lost" attend a church but have not personally committed their lives to Jesus Christ. This commitment, defined as confessing that Jesus is Lord (Rom 10:9-10), receiving his Holy Spirit as the seal of one's salvation (Eph 1:13-14) and experiencing a transformed life (1 Jn 5:3), is often called becoming "born again" (Jn 3:7; 1 Pet 1:22-23; 1 Jn 5:1) or "saved."

The churched lost coexist with saved church members but have failed to be personally converted to Christ. Jesus illustrated this in the stories of the goats that grow up with the sheep but then are not allowed to enter into the kingdom of God (Mt 25:32) and of the weeds that grow up with the wheat but in the end are separated out and burned (Mt 13:25-30). We are told that the churched lost will be shocked to discover their actual condition (Mt 25:41-45), for they often perceive themselves as every bit as good a Christian as anyone else.

Where are the churched lost? We find them in three types of
ecclesiastical settings: the most desperate group is found in the
false church; the highly confused group is found in the dead or
dying church; and those who are seeking are found in the living
church.

A false Christian church is not a Christian church at all. These
institutions move away from the orthodox tenets of Christianity,
becoming errant in their theology and teachings. Often the water-
shed issue that identifies a false church is the deity of Jesus Christ.
Heretical churches muddle up the person, work and sovereign
reign of Jesus Christ, transforming the biblical Jesus into something
less than God, making his salvation incomplete without the addition of their particular teachings.

Walter Martin's definitive *The Kingdom of the Cults* provides
extensive analysis of the origins and doctrines of these false Christian churches. Many use verbiage that appears to be Christian but
veils heretical doctrines that lie far outside the scope of the teachings of Christ. Such false churches include the Church of Jesus
Christ of Latter-day Saints, the Church of Scientology, the Worldwide Church of God, the Christian Science Church, the Way International, the Unitarian Universalist Church and the Unification
Church.

Parishioners from false churches are lost—perhaps more desperately so than those who attend no church at all. They truly
believe that their false church has found the secret keys to eternal
life when in fact they have been spiritually blinded and theologically duped. Concerns about transfer growth are not applicable
here; false church parishioners are fields in which the true church
is to be harvesting.

The second grouping of the churched lost are individuals who
are unsaved and attend historically Christian churches. The difficulty here lies in the term *historically*. Many Christian churches
and denominations have drifted away from the orthodox tenets of
the faith, retaining them in creed, on paper or in name only. In

practice, their teachings and positions do not reflect biblical truth. They are churches in transition, sliding from being Christian to offering unchristian teachings and values.

A problem exists, however, in clearly identifying which churches and denominations have stopped being Christian, thus making their members viable candidates for conversion and assimilation into other churches. The fact is, many sectors of Christendom contain the churched lost as a result of the church's loss of biblical orthodoxy. They are found in the Roman Catholic Church, the Orthodox churches, and Protestant churches, such as Episcopal, Methodist, Congregational (UCC), Baptist and other denominations. At the same time, in each of these denominations there are legitimate Christian pastors and church bodies that have experienced a personal relationship with the Lord Jesus Christ and uphold biblical teaching.

St. Paul's Episcopal Church in Darien, Connecticut, is an outstanding example of a believing community in a denomination that is in transition toward liberalism. We would be mistaken in assuming that the church is dead because of its denominational affiliation. This example highlights the need to discern the spiritual condition of "historical" Christian churches one church, one pastor, one person at a time. Otherwise we could be engaging in nothing more than transfer growth as we woo the saved to our church.

Another interesting question arises when we speak of reaching the churched lost in "historical" but now unorthodox Christian churches. Should we encourage those who become saved to leave these churches?

The easy answer is, of course we should! The church is dead, so we are saving people off a sinking ship. These new converts need discipleship, good teaching and proper care. Leaving them in a dead church could spell their doom. If we assimilate them, some would argue, we will be doing them a great service. Frankly, the sooner that dead church disappears, the better off the kingdom will be, for who knows how many people it will lure to their demise if it survives?

A tougher, more discerning answer requires kingdom eyes. How might we be a part of bringing life back into that dead church setting? Perhaps it occurs when members become saved and remain in their church, becoming the salt and light of the gospel. In this model, transfer growth is not the goal. Transferring the abundant life in Christ is.

Rescuing from Church Abuse

The third case in which transfer growth can be healthy involves a problem that is becoming more and more common in the Christian church: church abuse of parishioners.

Church abuse is a hideous crime. It occurs when churches or Christian leaders apply excessive control over parishioners in an effort to press them into loyalty, conformity and service. Such measures often leave damaged disciples, people broken by the very institution that promised to heal them. These individuals often have only one recourse for well-being: they must leave the abuse and discover a healthy church home.

The difficulty comes in defining what constitutes abuse. Is church discipline abuse? Or teaching about serious stewardship and tithing? What about calling for greater faith to receive more of the Spirit's power? Fine lines separate abusive teachings from the radical call of the gospel, and we must be aware that we will all have to live with the standards we establish.

In *Churches That Abuse* Ronald Enroth identifies five key areas where abuse commonly occurs. His categories can serve as a solid starting point when we are considering the validity of allowing a church transfer based on abuse: legalism, authoritarian leadership, manipulation, excessive discipline and spiritual intimidation.[8]

Legalism. Legalism is an unyielding application of the Scriptures; in abusive situations, a particular interpretation of biblical morality is applied without consideration of context, intent or proper exegetical principles. Such application works to create manipulative boundaries for people to become dependent on the leaders of the church to "interpret" the text. It creates an elitism that separates a church as special, proper and correct vis-à-vis the rest of the world.

Churches That Abuse tells how the verse "Come out and be separate" was turned into a legalistic call for elitism. "Pam and Tom's fellowship attempted to live according to first-century church standards. They believed the 'stain of the world' was upon the established church. Eventually this led to abuse as members were 'forced to cut all family ties and friendships outside of the fellowship.' Eventually some members realized this abuse, returning to their families. Such traitors were eternally condemned for not following the commands of God."[9] This is legalism, a mishandling of biblical texts that breaks the heart of God. Such abuse is wrong.

Leadership abuse. Authoritarian leadership invokes an extreme degree of control over the members of a church. By creating an unusual dependency on the leaders for all decision-making processes, the leaders become "God." Under the illusion that to disobey would bring terrible disaster, members are forced to live in suppression and fear.

"It reached a point," remembered one ex-member of a church community on the East Coast, "where the pastor just ruled your life. He told you where to live, whom to marry and what to give." This pastor demanded absolute respect. In a church softball game, after being called out on strikes, he became furious and demanded that "the scriptural double portion" for the priesthood be invoked so that he could gain three more opportunities to swing!

Such leaders consume people for personal gain. Money, sex and power are often the ulterior motives. The pastor in that East Coast church was sued by a disciple from whom he had tried to gain five million dollars. Eventually he lost the suit and was forced to rename his organization and move it to Baltimore to avoid further legal difficulties.

Manipulation. Manipulation is present in all the other forms of abuse; in Enroth's classification, however, manipulation involves a quest to elicit the people's agreement with the leader's position. It is abusive, for it often entails nothing short of blackmail.

Emmanuel Baptist Church had recently called a new pastor to its pulpit. As he visited his new parishioners, he would uncover information about the members of the church by saying, "Since I'm new to the flock . . . anything you could tell me about the people in the church would be of enormous help." In this fashion the pastor learned about "Mrs. Campbell's drinking problem, Frank Fowler's secret divorce, . . . and Brian Maguire's time in prison."[10]

The pastor then used the information for manipulative purposes. "When Frank Fowler demanded an agenda change during a church business meeting, the Pastor suggested a ten-minute break. 'You're being pretty tough on us, Frank. . . . I would think that a man who has made mistakes—especially marital ones—would be more compassionate."[11]

Severe discipline. Excessive disciplinary actions taken against nonconforming members is also abusive. In their milder forms, such measures may include ostracism from church activities; more aggressive actions involve verbal, physical and psychological torment.

A former member of the Centurion Door Church of Thousand Oaks, California, underwent extreme verbal abuse:

> [As] Paul continued to resist the indoctrinational process . . . "it became almost a daily ritual where I'd get called on the carpet . . . in what they called truth sessions. These sessions [which lasted two to three hours] . . . began with just a few persons, but evolved into hostile verbal beatings before the entire [church] group." Paul would be grilled, yelled at and screamed at until he finally [broke down and] began yelling and screaming at himself, rebuking Satan [in himself]. To stay sane . . . Paul yelled and screamed . . . even though he did not know what in the world was going on.[12]

Physical abuse was also a part of the Centurion Door's methods of discipleship. "There was punching, hitting, children were whipped with belts, and women were whipped with belts."[13] This abuse was done in the name of love and was given biblical credibility by an emphasis on certain Scriptures.

The Centurion's Door practiced psychological abuse as well. For example, women who were deemed unsubmissive to male authorities "were separated from their husbands and children until they repented."[14]

Often abusive churches employ spiritual intimidation to control their parishioners. Most notably, the Mormon Church practices severe acts of ostracism and spiritual damnation against any who desert the ranks. They and their families are unceremoniously pronounced cut from the Book of Life and condemned to hell for leaving the church.[15]

People coming out of cultlike groups calling themselves churches need desperately to feel the embrace of Christ's love. We must be sensitive in discerning the lines between abuse and biblical discipline in the church, but we must not tolerate or affirm violent or manipulative tactics that claim to represent the love of Christ. Enroth's categories of abuses can help us make wise assessments.

Life Is Messy

There is an inherent danger in any position that reflects inflexibility. The standard can seem unattainable at best and punitive at worst. Life is always messy. Rarely do situations arise that are readily solved through the process of plugging in a dogmatic, one-size-fits-all formula. Flexibility and the art of merging a principle with the realities of life are essential ingredients that need to be applied to the area of transfer growth if the church is to succeed in addressing this issue.

This statement may seem antithetical to the positions thus far established in this book. My insistence of high standards is a direct response to the wanton low standards that are now the norm. Frankly, I feel that a wake up call needed to be issued, one that graphically contrasted the stark reality of where we are with the biblical standards of where we need to be.

In the following three examples I have attempted to show incidents where transfer growth may occur apart from rescuing sheep and still produce health in the body of Christ. The examples serve only to show that transfer growth often needs careful, pastoral supervision. My hope is that these illustrations will capture the integrity of this book's message and help churches practically apply its principles when hard calls require wisdom and a pastoral heart.

Leadership Changes

For many people Sunday worship defines the most important level of involvement in their relationship to a local church. Here they are fed, and often the decision to stay or leave a church is based on the leadership's ability to meet their needs during the worship service.

When leadership changes frequently, a person's loyalty to a given church is challenged. "I have never felt close to the new pastor," said Thomas. "His sermons and style just don't appeal to me. I need to be somewhere that will encourage me spiritually. This change in pastoral staff has inspired my decision to leave the church and shop for a new one." Thomas continued, "Since we have been attending this new church I have shared Christ with an employee because of the inspirational teaching I am now receiving. I haven't ever shared my faith before. This new church is definitely where I need and want to be." He concluded, "I don't feel guilty about leaving my old church. From my perspective my pastor left me, freeing me to find another church."

Addressing the issue of transfer growth as the result of leadership changes is an important topic to discuss, because it happens often. For Thomas, pastoral desertion inspired his move. That certainly is a dilemma that challenges the axiom of just sending him back to his old church. In a very real sense, his old church is gone. When the new pastor simply was not connecting with Thomas's world, a problem arose that he couldn't fix. It was not Thomas's fault, nor was there some sinister evil behind his motives. Circumstances simply changed that greatly affected his Christian experience.

How do we respond to a Thomas? Recently I let a Thomas stay based on several pastoral motivations. This young man was desperate for growth, and our church was able to meet his needs and his family's needs powerfully. His pain from the loss of his pastor was evident, and he clearly felt that he needed to find a church setting to which he could relate. He was not angry, just disconnected—like a sheep without a shepherd—and he needed a home.

Having said this, let me be quick to point out that this process of staying at our church involved several things from Thomas. First, Thomas needed to address his reasons for leaving his church in person. A letter avoids dialogue, and sometimes direct contact can be instrumental in helping someone who is disconnected to find a connection again. Plus the church has the right to know why he left. Perhaps it will help them address issues that are being overlooked, improving their program.

Second, Thomas needed to understand that his perception of the church was limited in scope, which adversely affected his ability to feel connected with the body. The church is not an individual. In our agreement Thomas and his wife agreed to be a part of a small group in order to help him discover that the Sunday experience is just one facet (and for many in our church the least significant facet) of what it means to belong to a church. We needed to be deliberate in helping Thomas discover a new depth to his relationship with the church. Thomas needed to discover relationships and the joy of becoming an intimate part of the body of Christ.

Third, we spoke honestly. Thomas and his wife were obviously surprised that I suggested returning to their church of origin, and they were a bit overwhelmed with my systematic approach of developing goals for them if they chose to stay. In this situation I took the time to educate this couple about the fact that church hopping was killing the kingdom, and that they needed to weigh heavily their contribution to this problem. They had to consider what the best solution was for them and for the kingdom of God. Then when they made a decision, they needed to work hard at developing a long-term commitment that would help them avoid repeating this process in the future.

The final goal of this process was to curb the flow of transfer growth, both in the present and in the future, while meeting the needs of God's people. In this case the goal was realized.

A Philosophy of Ministry Shift

Sometimes pastoral decisions regarding transfer growth flow in the other direction. When is it appropriate to let people go?

I think one of the most common situations in which letting people go is justified is when an obvious shift in philosophy of ministry occurs, creating a set of goals and objectives for the church which may not address a particular individual's needs. Pragmatically this often happens when a church begins to grow. The old guard is often challenged by the new people, and as the numerical balance of the congregation shifts, so do the bulk of the decisions in favor of the new agenda. Conflict may result with people feeling that they just do not fit in to the "new" ministry.

In a perfect world this would never occur, but even with the purest of hearts a change in the philosophy of ministry can greatly affect an individual's ability to relate to and be a part of a body. Good pastoring skills can make this difficult process better for everyone involved. Key among those skills is being able to let people go with a blessing.

When I arrived at Stroudwater the church desired to grow and reach young people; this was the expressed concern of the church board. I tried to explain some of the cost involved in this new philosophy of ministry, including the dramatic changes that would take place. Everyone seemed willing to take on the challenge.

However, nothing prepares people for the shock of change.

When the organ is sold and a worship team brought in, when someone is sitting in your pew or when the greeters ask a charter member if they would like a visitor's packet, the shock of change is felt! Change can be difficult, and in the process of a church changing, some people will desire to leave.

As our church focused on the young families, we moved further and further away from meeting the needs of our seniors and retired couples. Many of them called and spoke to me about their need for fellowship, but our church just could not produce the experience for which they were longing. Then one couple found a lovely church in the city that specifically focused on their age bracket. Soon I knew that several of our seniors were visiting this church and that they were having their needs met in important ways that we could not reproduce.

To their credit, these folks called me and shared their need for change. Ironically, it was the church's success that was the reason for leaving, but they still had needs too. Many of them had stayed longer than they wanted to, making sure that we were financially able to survive before they talked with me. I hated to see them go, but these saints deserved to have a place that provided the rich hymns and bean suppers for them that they loved!

In each of these cases I expressed my support for their decision to leave and a deep appreciation for their support to our church. In these situations transfer growth was a timely and proper way of expressing the love of Christ. The fruit of this wisdom can be found in the pews of our church where many of their adult children now worship and where they often return to visit.

A Second Chance

There are situations where transfer growth provides a setting for people that allows them the opportunity to start over again. Although I do not support escapism, there can be specific instances where a change is needed for an individual's personal development.

Kris and Ronnie had struggled in their marriage for many years. Both wanted to love the Lord, yet in their marriage they were drifting farther and farther apart. The church they were attending became the focus of much of their time. Kris worked long hours with the youth, and Ronnie was actively involved in the worship services. It was in this environment that one of them began to have an affair with another member of the church.

When the affair became known the couple struggled, both personally and corporately. Personally they needed help in repairing their marriage. Corporately they needed a loving environment where they could find counsel and support.

The church they were attending was deeply affected by the incident. It was a small church, and quite naturally, many members felt the pain and repercussions of the situation. It soon became evident that this would be a very difficult setting for the couple to remain in if they were going to experience healing, so they transferred to another church.

To their credit, they expressed to their old church their reasons for leaving. Key elements included the fact that the church was not to blame and that they accepted the responsibility of having brought much grief to the congregation through the trauma of the affair. They clearly shared that for both parties the decision to separate would be an important element in helping the healing to begin.

For Ronnie and Kris, a new setting did provide the support that they needed. They were honest with the pastoral staff of the new church and explained clearly the situation and their need for help. They submitted to oversight and participated in counseling and training. Today they are a new couple with a wonderful testimony that reflects the love that Christ invested in them. They believe that the church transfer was a life-giving element in saving their marriage. In this case I think they were right.

Conclusion

Today we are confronted with the reality that the church has stopped growing. That needs to be an alarming concern for the church, and it needs to present a challenge to the way we have been operating. Funny, the "seven last words of a dying church"—"We've never done it that way before"—may well end up on the tombstone of the church growth movement and the evangelical community if we do not adopt new standards for seeking growth. It is time to begin. Growing into a community of depth and character is the challenge facing the church of the new millennium.

EPILOGUE

The LORD is my shepherd, I shall not be in want.
   He makes me lie down in green pastures,
he leads me beside quiet waters,
   he restores my soul.
He guides me in paths of righteousness
   for his name's sake. PSALM 23:1-3

She was not much to look at anymore. Her features were weathered, and the years of abandonment had taken their toll. Her original purpose had all but been forgotten as men tinkered with her soul in a vain attempt to get her to regain her fallen glory. There she sat alone, cold and destined for the junkyard.

Yet I bought her, a vintage 1980 MG. She once had been the hallmark of the sports-car world, winning international acclaim in rally racing and providing inspiration for designers of later model cars. Even though she had not run in nearly a decade, I knew she wanted to. Every line on that car cried out for the open road.

And so it is with the church, and the timeless message of which it is the keeper. To us has been revealed the secret wisdom of God, a wisdom, as Paul writes, "that has been hidden and that God destined for our glory before time began" (1 Cor 2:7). It is the secret of a God who still seeks to save the lost (Lk 19:10) and still longs for his stewards to be investing boldly for his kingdom (Mt 25:14-30). This message sits patiently under the hood of the church, just waiting for the bold congregation that will restore it.

Clearly the church has suffered a stall in advancing the good news that Jesus Christ provides an eternal home for those who receive him as their Lord and Savior. Some would argue that the base percentages of conversions have remained constant for centuries and that nothing is wrong, but that is of little comfort when we become aware of the vast increases in professionally trained clergy and powerful church growth tools that have been employed in recent years. We should be doing a better job of reaching the lost, and perhaps the difference between success and failure is a simple adjustment.

The MG's odometer pointed to a problem. Seeing scarcely enough miles on her for a year of driving, and scanning a paper trail of quick sales, I knew no one could get the MG to run. Cars usually have one of two problems, electrical failure or fuel problems. She had spark but no gas. Systematically I replaced the gas tank, fuel pump, filters, sending units and gas lines, until I arrived at the carburetor.

Initially it appeared fine, but after an afternoon of false starts, further examination revealed a simple mistake that was killing the car. The floats had been installed by a previous mechanic upside down. Anxiously I made this minor correction—and the MG immediately barked to life. By spring she will once again be experiencing her former glory.

The church, too, has spark but no gas. Our engines churn and we make a mighty sound, but we are failing to move ahead in both spiritual depth and evangelistic productivity. Our focus has mysteriously been tinkered with and reinstalled upside down. Could it be that with one simple adjustment—sincerely focusing on the unsaved and developing Christian maturity— the church could regain its former glory? There is no question in my mind that these are the keys.

It is exciting to imagine a world in which all the wonderful tools of church growth are focused on the harvest and in which the tools are employed according to our highest moral standards. We have been given so much—thousand and thousands of hours of research and techniques that really do help the church to grow. For the love of our God, let us use this vast array of knowledge in an effort to turn around the flat growth lines and the rotting moral standards of the church. Let us major in the harvest, with integrity in all our processes.

I am optimistic that the church is facing a new era of growth. It is time for the church to be proactive and to manage its programs aggressively, assessing accurately and precisely who the intended audience is and what the outcome of each program should be. This is the season of the last days, and we more than any other generation should be bold investors of our talents for the kingdom, not naysayers at the fringes of the will of God. I believe God's attitude regarding the church's outreach is captured in these words of Teddy Roosevelt:

It is not the critic who counts. . . . The credit belongs to the man in the arena whose face is marred by dust and sweat and blood . . . who at best knows [in the end] the triumph of high achievement and who at worst, if he fails, fails while daring greatly, so that his place will never be with those cold timid souls who never knew victory or defeat.[1]

May God grant us the honor of mastering the tools of reaching our fallen world that we might move "further up and further in" to the heart of God. A biblical passion for the lost, thoughtfully channeled, will lead us into the paths of righteousness and the still waters that bless those who discover his pleasure.

Notes

Chapter 1: Stealing Sheep

[1] C. Peter Wagner, Carl George and Charles Kraft have all stated that fat sheep don't wander. I think they do. It has to do primarily with the American consumer mentality.

[2] Richard Peace, lecture notes for Exegeting the Culture, Fuller Theological Seminary, Pasadena, Calif., May 10, 1995.

[3] Ibid.

[4] Cornel West, "The '80s Market Culture Run Amok," *Newsweek,* January 3, 1994, p. 48.

[5] See C. Peter Wagner, *Understanding Church Growth,* 3rd ed. (Grand Rapids, Mich.: Eerdmans, 1990), pp. 47-48. It must be emphasized that Winter's original categories were based on evangelism that produced conversions. Church growth discipleship programs also use elements of this model (D-1, D-2, D-3; see chapter two of Win Arn and Charles Arn, *The Master's Plan for Making Disciples* [Monrovia, Calif.: Church Growth, 1982]). However, we have ended up with a model for sheep stealing.

The homogeneous unit principle, articulated by Donald McGavran, noted that evangelistic efforts within family networks are far more productive in producing converts than the individual methods employed by the missions organizations of his day. Interestingly, contemporary web-of-influence theories have mostly just enlarged upon McGavran's principle.

[6] Churches and denominations have considered each other's members fair game for conversion, albeit not conversion in the evangelistic sense of the word, for centuries. Conversions to different points of theology, traditions and styles have often been justified as reasons for a person to change churches. This form of stealing for the sake of growth is a relatively common practice often occurring between Catholic, Protestant and Orthodox churches.

[7] This is one of the blind spots that have encouraged sheep stealing. Accurate assessments—a standard for church growth—had not been devised to plot conversion growth. In other words, numerical growth was the goal; conversions were assumed! (See note 34 in chapter three.)

[8] Paul Borthwick's *A Mind for Missions* (Colorado Springs: NavPress, 1987), p. 32, establishes the case for missions beginning with the premise Jesus commissioned us to tell the world that salvation can be found solely in him. "Through His Son, God demonstrates His sending heart; He reaches out to lost humanity by giving the only sacrifice that will satisfy the Law and restore a right relationship between man and God. Jesus Christ, God's divine Son, is sent so that 'whoever believes in Him shall not perish but have eternal life' (John 3:16). . . . In the gospels the missionary God reveals Himself through His Son who is not only sent, but also sends

His followers in a renewed commission. . . . The commission is clear—so clear that all four gospel writers recorded it in one form or another (and Luke recorded it again in Acts 1:8): Matt. 28:19—'Therefore go and make disciples of all the nations'; Mark 16:15—'go into all the world and preach the good news to all creation'; Luke 24:47—'Repentance and forgiveness of sins will be preached in His name to all nations'; John 20:21—'As the Father has sent me, I am sending you.'" This is the evangelical position on the task of the church as the proactive arm of God in the world today, under the direction of the Holy Spirit, reconciling a lost world to its Creator.

9Carl F. George, *Prepare Your Church for the Future* (Grand Rapids, Mich.: Revell, 1993), pp. 31-32. George, who claims C. Peter Wagner as his mentor, has some strong opinions about the process of sheep stealing. In this section of George's book he actually takes the position that there are small "feeder churches" whose function and lot in life is to be drained of their constituents by bigger and better churches. The smaller traditional churches cannot keep up with the progress of church growth churches, and they in essence become the sources for the growth of the "receptor" churches. Such aggressive behavior deeply divides churches. (See appendix D of George's book.)

10Donald McGavran, "Sheep Stealing and Church Growth," in *The Pastor's Church Growth Handbook,* ed. Win Arn (Pasadena, Calif.: Church Growth, 1979), p. 18.

11Ibid., pp. 17-18.

12Donald McGavran and C. Peter Wagner, *Your Church and Church Growth: A Self-Study Course,* rev. ed. (Pasadena, Calif.: Charles E. Fuller Institute of Evangelism and Church Growth, 1982), p. 6.

13David F. Wells, *God in the Wasteland* (Grand Rapids, Mich.: Eerdmans, 1994), p. 77.

14From McGavran and Wagner, *Your Church and Church Growth,* side B of audiotape 1.

15Os Guinness states, "Once a growing church reaches the critical mass of one thousand, the sky is the limit for its financial and organizational potential for future growth through a myriad of dazzling modern insights and technologies" (*Dining with the Devil* [Grand Rapids, Mich.: Baker, 1993], p. 12).

16Don Baker, *Beyond Forgiveness* (Portland, Ore.: Multnomah Press, 1984), pp. 83-84.

17C. Peter Wagner, "A Glossary of Church Growth Terms," in *Church Growth: State of the Art,* ed. C. Peter Wagner (Wheaton, Ill.: Tyndale House, 1986), p. 300.

18Philip Kenneson and James Street, *Selling Out of the Church* (Nashville: Abingdon, 1997), p. 17, lists twelve different types of motivations for churches and ministries that are less than biblical; according to the authors, these motivations reflect negative aspects of modernity.

Chapter 2: Bleating Sheep
1Robert Patterson, "In Search of the Visible Church," *Christianity Today,* March 11, 1991, p. 36.

2Charles Colson and Ellen Santilli Vaughn, *The Body* (Dallas: Word, 1992), p. 30.

3Charles Van Engen, *God's Missionary People* (Grand Rapids, Mich.: Baker, 1995), p. 15.

[4]John Paul II, *Crossing the Threshold of Hope* (New York: Alfred A. Knopf, 1994), p. 3.

[5]Quoted in Richard John Neuhaus, *Freedom for Ministry* (Grand Rapids, Mich.: Eerdmans, 1992), p. 54.

[6]O. Linton, *ekklēsia,* in *Theological Dictionary of the New Testament,* ed. Gerhard Kittel and Gerhard Friedrich, trans. G. W. Bromiley, 10 vols. (Grand Rapids, Mich.: Eerdmans, 1965), 3:501-13.

[7]1 Corinthians 12; 1 Peter 2:9. Carl F. H. Henry, "Churches and Christian Fellowship," *Basic Biblical Beliefs: Six Foundational Christian Doctrines,* pt. 5, teaching sessions, in Charles Colson and Ellen Santilli Vaughn, *The Body* (Dallas: Word, 1992), p. 66.

[8]The Nicene Creed, in Anthony M. Coniaris, *Introducing the Orthodox Church* (Minneapolis: Light and Life, 1982), p. 16.

[9]Van Engen, *God's Missionary People,* p. 16.

[10]Colson and Vaughn, *The Body,* p. 69.

[11]Ibid., p. 68.

[12]Paul Minear, *Images of the Church in the New Testament* (Philadelphia: Westminster Press, 1977).

[13]Robert Laird Harris, *Theological Wordbook of the Old Testament* (Chicago: Moody Press, 1981), p. 661.

[14]Bob Slosser, *Miracle in Darien* (Plainfield, N.J.: Logos International, 1979), pp. 117-18.

[15]Robert N. Bellah et al., *Habits of the Heart: Individualism and Commitment in American Life* (Berkeley: University of California Press, 1985), p. 84.

[16]Some readers may wonder why I have not returned to my original church. Am I being inconsistent with my own views? In my case the Catholic church I attended did not have leadership who had experienced a personal relationship with the Lord. That means the church was not the body of Christ but more of a social club, a traditional religious part of our community's life. As a new Christian I had a desperate need for fellowship and discipleship, and this environment simply could not address these issues. At this juncture I sought out a body of believers who could help me grow in my new faith. When we find ourselves in a non-Christian environment, there is no conflict with the principles of transfer growth that we have discussed. Instead, our concern rests in how we address the actual body of Christ.

We all experience a learning curve as we examine appropriate responses to situations that traditionally have been rectified by leaving a church. Praxis as related to sheep stealing comes through discovering the Spirit's leading in regard to the quintessential pastoral question, What is a godly response to transfer growth? Our learning curve demands discovery, conviction and accountability, with each individual and church asking the question, "What does God want us to do?" Our responses may vary, but being sensitive and aware of the true impact of our decisions is a nonnegotiable responsibility for all who are called to be disciples of Christ. I believe that once we see the damaging impact of sheep stealing we will never be able to engage in it casually again. The Holy Spirit will cause us to develop new standards by which to live.

[17]John Calvin, *Institutes of the Christian Religion,* ed. J. T. McNeill, 2 vols. (Philadelphia: Westminster Press, 1960), 2:1012.

[18]Neuhaus, *Freedom for Ministry,* p. 53.

[19]Van Engen, *God's Missionary People,* p. 69.

[20]Howard A. Snyder, *The Community of the King* (Downers Grove, Ill.: InterVarsity Press, 1977), p. 74.

[21]Ibid., p. 197.

[22]Minear, *Images of the Church,* pp. 193-94.

Chapter 3: Have You Any Wool?

[1]David Wells, *God in the Wasteland* (Grand Rapids, Mich.: Eerdmans, 1994), p. 68.

[2]C. Peter Wagner, *Church Growth and the Whole Gospel: A Biblical Mandate* (San Francisco: Harper & Row, 1981), p. 11.

[3]James D. Berkley, "Church Growth Comes of Age," *Leadership* 12 (Fall 1991): 108-15.

[4]Rodger C. Bassham, *Mission Theology, 1948-1975: Years of Worldwide Creative Tension—Ecumenical, Evangelical and Roman Catholic* (Pasadena, Calif.: William Carey Library, 1979), p. 198.

[5]Paul Yonggi Cho, *Successful Home Cell Groups* (South Plainfield, N.J.: Bridge, 1981), p. 6.

[6]*Megachurch* is the church growth term for an individual congregation that has more than two thousand members. Leith Anderson characterizes megachurches as those that have "large staffs, require expansive facilities, operate on multimillion dollar budgets, provide an impressive variety of services, tend to be leader led, and often have excellent preaching and music" (*A Church for the Twenty-first Century* [Minneapolis: Bethany House, 1992], p. 54). Such size was fairly rare in Protestant churches until the advent of the church growth movement. Today a growing number of churches in the United States have achieved this benchmark (see Edythe Draper, ed., *The Almanac of the Christian World* [Wheaton, Ill.: Tyndale House, 1990]).

Metachurches "are based on a network of small groups that function as centers for assimilation, training, pastoral care, and evangelism. Each group has a leader but also trains another leader in anticipation of generating another small group. They are decentralized into homes, offices, and other meeting places. Because so much ministry is lay led and small-group based, the professional staff of the metachurch may be very small" (Anderson, *Church for the Twenty-first Century,* p. 55). The largest example of a metachurch is the remarkable Full Gospel Central Church of Seoul. Although most of the church functions on a small group or cell group level, as a pragmatic necessity all are encouraged to attend Sunday worship services using a unique rotation schedule.

[7]Donald McGavran, *The Bridges of God: A Study in the Strategy of Missions* (London: World Dominion, 1955), p. 158.

[8]At this time (1991) Wagner stopped writing church growth material, refocusing his energies on the work of prayer in world evangelization.

[9]"Decadal growth rate" (DGR) is defined by the church growth movement (see C. Peter Wagner, ed., *Church Growth: State of the Art* [Wheaton, Ill.: Tyndale House, 1986], p. 287) as the net increase in church membership over an entire decade expressed in percentage.

[10]George Barna, news release, Barna Research Group, February 28, 1996, p. 2.

[11]Ibid.

[12]Doug Murren, *The Baby Boomerang* (Ventura, Calif.: Regal, 1990), p. 10.

[13]Barna, news release, p. 1.

[14]Conversion growth is the numerical increase of a church that results from individuals' acknowledging a personal faith in Jesus Christ for the first time. It is this form of church expansion that is clearly anticipated by Jesus in the Great Commission (Mt 28:19-20).

[15]D. James Kennedy, *Evangelism Explosion* (Wheaton, Ill.: Tyndale House, 1983).

[16]Rick Warren, *The Purpose-Driven Church* (Grand Rapids, Mich.: Zondervan, 1995), focuses on the target character of Saddleback Sam in chapter nine.

[17]Lee Strobel, *Inside the Mind of Unchurched Harry and Mary* (Grand Rapids, Mich.: Zondervan, 1993), describes Willow Creek's evangelistic programming in great detail.

[18]See Mark 13:26-27: "At that time men will see the Son of Man coming in clouds with great power and glory. And he will send his angels and gather his elect from the four winds, from the ends of the earth to the ends of the heavens."

[19]See 1 Thessalonians 4:16-18: "For the Lord himself will come down from heaven, with a loud command, with the voice of the archangel and with the trumpet call of God, and the dead in Christ will rise first. After that, we who are still alive and are left will be caught up together with them in the clouds to meet the Lord in the air. And so we will be with the Lord forever. Therefore encourage each other with these words."

[20]Kingdom growth is conversion growth. When people accept Jesus as Lord and make a profession of faith, a soul is added to the book of life and the kingdom of God grows.

[21]Wagner, *Church Growth and the Whole Gospel*, p. 10.

[22]There were six students in my group, each recording thirty surveys, for a total of 180 surveys. A 9 percent survey test group is considered very good.

[23]Jack Hayford, endorsement on the dust jacket of Ted Haggard, *Primary Purpose: Making It Hard For People From Your City to Go to Hell* (Lake Mary, Fla.: Creation House, 1995).

[24]Haggard, *Primary Purpose,* p. 84.

[25]Ibid., p. 87.

[26]Peter Kaldor et al., *The Winds of Change: The Experience of Church in a Changing Australia* (Sydney: Anzea, 1994), pp. 207-8.

[27]Ibid., p. 226.

[28]Ibid., p. 227.

[29]Ibid.

[30]Ibid., p. 239.

[31]Ibid., p. 227.

[32]Ibid., p. 229.

[33]Ibid., p. 230.

Chapter 4: Counting Sheep

[1]Ronald F. Youngblood, "1, 2 Samuel," in *The Expositor's Bible Commentary,* ed. Frank E. Gaebelein (Grand Rapids, Mich.: Zondervan, 1992), 3:1096. "The arena of David's transgression appears to be that taking a census impugns the faithfulness of God in the keeping of His promises—a kind of walking by sight instead of by faith" (Raymond B. Dillard, "David's Census: Perspectives on 2 Samuel 24 and

1 Chronicles 21," in *Through Christ's Word: A Festschrift for Dr. Philip E. Hughes,* ed. W. Robert Godfrey and Jesse L. Boyd III [Phillipsburg, N.J.: Presbyterian & Reformed, 1985], pp. 104-5).

[2]Ralph Earle, "1 Timothy," in *Expositor's Bible Commentary,* 11:385. "Eager is the present participle of the *orego* (cf. 1 Timothy 3:1)—always 'reaching after, grasping at.' . . . This is the curse of too much of modern living. Some Christians, unfortunately, have been trapped in this way. They have 'wandered' (*a peplanethesan,* 'been led astray,' only here and Mark 13:22) from the faith. In straying from the straight path, they have been caught in the thorn bushes and have 'pierced themselves with many griefs' (*odynais,* only here and Romans 9:2). Another translation is: 'They have pierced themselves to the heart with many pangs.'"

[3]Hans-Reudi Weber, "God's Arithmetic," *Frontier* 6 (Winter 1963): 298.

[4]C. René Padilla, "A Steep Climb Ahead for Theology in Latin America," *Evangelical Missions Quarterly* 7, no. 2 (1971): 104.

[5]Ralph P. Martin, "Church Growth Is Not the Point," *Life of Faith,* January 10, 1976.

[6]Donald A. McGavran, *The Bridges of God: A Study in the Strategy of Missions* (London: World Dominion, 1955), p. 127.

[7]Dean R. Hoge and David A. Roozen, eds., *Understanding Church Growth and Decline, 1950-1978* (New York: Pilgrim, 1979), p. 315.

[8]Bob Waymire and C. Peter Wagner, *The Church Growth Survey Handbook* (Milpitas, Calif.: Global Church Growth, 1984), provides helpful charts, graphs and procedures for recording and analyzing church growth. This material has been standard church growth issue for over twenty years. One of the primary dispensers of this and all the church growth materials has been the Charles E. Fuller Institute of Church Growth, located just off the campus of Fuller Seminary in Pasadena, California.

[9]Padilla, "Steep Climb Ahead," pp. 102, 104.

[10]The next chapter will develop the history of sheep stealing and explore how it was that numbers became such an important focus in the process of growing churches.

[11]Os Guinness, *Dining with the Devil* (Grand Rapids, Mich.: Baker, 1993), p. 49.

[12]Gordon Fee, *The First Epistle to the Corinthians,* New International Commentary on the New Testament (Grand Rapids, Mich.: Eerdmans, 1987), p. 145.

[13]Jack Hayford, "How Many Did You Have Last Sunday?" *Leadership,* Winter 1998, p. 39.

[14]The church growth movement holds up Acts 2:42 as a description of the daily functioning of the churches that grew out of Peter's Pentecost sermon. Each of them seemed to produce the fruit of conversions,: "And the Lord added to their number daily those who were being saved" (Acts 2:47). This accords with the commission issued by the Lord in Matthew 28:19-20.

[15]C. Peter Wagner, *Church Growth and the Whole Gospel: A Biblical Mandate* (San Francisco: Harper & Row, 1981), p. 73.

[16]Charles Van Engen, *God's Missionary People: Rethinking the Purpose of the Local Church* (Grand Rapids, Mich.: Baker, 1995), p. 81.

[17]C. Peter Wagner, lecture notes for Church Growth I, Fuller Theological Seminary, March 4, 1991.

[18]McGavran, *Bridges of God,* p. 48.

19Ibid., p. 49.
20Ibid., p. 50.
21Ibid., pp. 51-52.
22Ibid., p. 53.
23Ibid.
24Ibid.
25Ibid.
26Ibid., p. 5.
27Ibid., pp. 54-55.
28Waymire and Wagner, *Church Growth Survey Handbook,* p. 1.
29McGavran, *Bridges of God;* see chapter 11, "Research in Growth," and chapter 9, "Important Aspects of This Dynamic Strategy." Here McGavran uses growth percentages to determine the health of a church or mission station.
30Donald A. McGavran, *Understanding Church Growth* (Grand Rapids, Mich.: Eerdmans, 1970), p. 67.
31McGavran, *Bridges of God,* p. 109.
32"The older churches need to regard their present buildings on the one hand as expendable and on the other as dedicated to the business of witnessing for Christ in the places where they have been built. 'We probed for seventy years', the older churches might say, 'and explored a great new territory. We built the kind of a base which could have served a mighty Christward movement. However, such an exodus did not occur here. It did arise 250 miles away. We refused to be tied down by this base to a scheme which is non-productive as regards the discipling of peoples. We shall turn this plant over. . . . They have rendered their service—*a wonderful service.* But we shall not let them sway our thinking in the vital matters ahead of us'" (*Bridges of God,* p. 147). Here one gains the sense of McGavran's quest for productivity and his pragmatic response to churches that had apparently lost their evangelical value. A similar lack of concern for other churches shows up in the act of soliciting members from ministries that are "dying" or that are simply not as productive as one's own.
33Wagner, "Biblical Principles," lecture notes for Church Growth I, Fuller Theological Seminary, March 6, 1991.
34Wagner, "Biblical Principles for Strategy Planning," lecture notes for Church Growth I, Fuller Theological Seminary, 1991, p. 2.
35Lesslie Newbigin, *The Open Secret: Sketches for a Missionary Theology* (Grand Rapids, Mich.: Eerdmans, 1978), p. 142.
36Years later I saw this man receive a regional award acknowledging his church's growth and contribution to evangelistic efforts in our area. Numerical growth is often the measure by which our peers judge our ministry.
37McGavran, *Bridges of God,* pp. 144-45.
38Donald McGavran and C. Peter Wagner, *Your Church and Church Growth: A Self-Study Course,* rev. ed. (Pasadena, Calif.: Charles E. Fuller Institute of Evangelism and Church Growth, 1982), p. 6 in the workbook and tape 1 argue the validity of taking sheep from other churches if their needs are not being met.
39Quoted in a Wagner lecture in Church Growth I, March 7, 1991.
40Carl F. George, *Prepare Your Church for the Future* (Grand Rapids, Mich.: Revell), p. 31.
41Ibid., p. 97.

[42]David Wells, *God in the Wasteland* (Grand Rapids, Mich.: Eerdmans, 1994), p. 73.

[43]Ted Haggard, *Primary Purpose: Making It Hard for People from Your City to Go to Hell* (Orlando: Creation House, 1995), pp. 84-85.

[44]Wagner has stopped producing church growth materials, and has started focusing on spiritual warfare and apostolic ministry issues. Interestingly, this realignment coincides with his discovery of the flat growth line that he announced to our Church Growth class in 1991.

[45]Waymire and Wagner's *Church Growth Survey Handbook* is the primary step-by-step workbook for basic church growth analysis. In it the composite membership of a church constitutes the actual number of individuals who effectively are involved with any given ministry. Church membership, worship attendance and adult Sunday school attendance are used as follows: "If, for example, membership is 400, worship attendance is 300, and Sunday School is 200, composite would be 300 (400 + 300 + 200 = 900 divided by 3 = 300)." The purpose of finding the composite membership of a church is to reduce the effect of inaccurate and inflated statistics so that a "truer" picture of the church's people involvement can be determined. Unfortunately, transfers can readily be assimilated into the composite formula, so it does not reveal actual kingdom growth statistics.

[46]In recent years the church growth movement has begun to give attention to statistical information regarding "conversion growth." Perhaps in part due to awareness of stagnant growth curves, more concern is being generated to refocus the movement on the primary purpose of reaching the lost.

Chapter 5: Fleecing the Flock

[1]Ted Haggard, *Primary Purpose: Making It Hard for People from Your City to Go to Hell* (Orlando, Fla.: Creation House, 1995), p. 87.

[2]Kennon L. Callahan, *Twelve Keys to an Effective Church: The Planning Workbook* (San Francisco: Harper & Row, 1983), p. 5.

[3]When is it healthy to leave a church? There are several situations that merit an individual's departure from a fellowship. Abuse of many types is a valid reason. Heretical teaching that is dogmatic and absolute creates an unhealthy church environment, which is best avoided. Sometimes individuals will be confronted with ministries that are one-dimensional and not open to change or growth, stagnating their members. These restrictive environments sometimes merit change. I am sure that there are many other reasons for transfer that can be justified and are legitimate, but I want to strongly emphasize that the highest and best good in many situations is to work out the problems together, growing in the Lord along the way. Transferring is too often the cheap fix when working out the problems would be a more productive long-term solution for that setting and for the kingdom.

[4]In New Life's defense, this is one of the best transfer-to-conversion ratios I found in my research. Other large churches claim to have succeeded in experiencing only twenty percent through transfers, but I sense that may be overly optimistic. Our church struggles to keep the ratio at twenty-five percent in spite of our very conscious efforts to avoid sheep stealing. This merely points to the pervasiveness of this problem.

[5]Philemon is a letter that richly portrays this concept.

[6]David Goetz, "Tour of Duty," *Leadership* 17, Spring 1996, p. 23.

[7]National Clergy Support Network, P.O. Box 52044, Raleigh, North Carolina 27612; information available at <www.concentric.net/~Pstrcare/>.

[8]Report of Superintendent Clinton E. Taber, Eastern Regional Association, Advent Christian General Conference, October 16, 1998, p. 18.

[9]"It is well to remember that the modern ecumenical movement grew out of a genuine evangelistic and missionary concern. But with time, it broke from its biblical and theological moorings and largely went astray. Because of this, many evangelicals practically equate ecumenism with heresy" (Howard A. Snyder, *The Community of the King* [Downers Grove, Ill.: InterVarsity Press, 1977], p. 204).

[10]Donald G. Bloesch, *The Reform of the Church* (Grand Rapids, Mich.: Eerdmans, 1970), p. 184.

[11]D. James Kennedy, *Evangelism Explosion* (Wheaton, Ill.: Tyndale House, 1983), p. 9.

[12]Snyder, *Community of the King*, p. 175.

[13]C. Peter Wagner, "Biblical Principles," lecture notes for Church Growth I, Pasadena, Calif.: Fuller Theological Seminary, March 7, 1991, p. 2.

[14]C. S. Lewis, *The Screwtape Letters* (New York: Macmillan, 1961), p. 156.

[15]David Wells, *God in the Wasteland* (Grand Rapids, Mich.: Eerdmans, 1994), pp. 85-86.

[16]Os Guinness, *Dining with the Devil* (Grand Rapids, Mich.: Baker, 1993), p. 49.

[17]Peter L. Berger, *A Rumor of Angels* (New York: Anchor, 1990), p. 25.

[18]Wagner, "Biblical Principles," lecture notes for Church Growth I, March 11, 1991, p. 2.

[19]David F. Wells, *Losing Our Virtue* (Grand Rapids, Mich.: Eerdmans, 1998), p. 4.

[20]Gene A. Getz, *Building Up One Another* (Wheaton, Ill.: Scripture Press, 1976), p. 5.

[21]I was so moved by his appreciation and the rightness of what we had accomplished that since that time Carol and I have invited two other pastors into our small group, equipping them to bring community to their churches. This is a powerful model for strength in the pastoral ministry—not just sharing small groups but giving away all your special talents and skills to others who need them. It strengthens the church and brings harmony to the body.

[22]No doubt a long and fruitless debate could ensue here. Many branches of Christendom do not acknowledge that a Catholic can be a Christian or that an Orthodox priest can know Christ. That simply is not true, and the church will have to grow up in its understanding that the central issue in salvation is our Christology. Beyond that our differences will probably always exist, but they should never give us permission to abuse each other. In my travels in countries that are hostile to the gospel, I have seen that the Christian churches stick together. In the face of persecution a clearer vision is quickly gained.

[23]Matthew Arnold, "Stanzas from the Grand Chartreuse" (1855).

[24]William D. Hendricks, *Exit Interviews* (Chicago: Moody Press, 1993), p. 70.

[25]Dietrich Bonhoeffer, *Life Together* (San Francisco: Harper & Row, 1954), p. 17.

[26]William E. Hordern reviews Bonhoeffer's concept of cheap grace in *A Layman's Guide to Protestant Theology* (New York: Macmillan, 1955), pp. 213-14.

[27]James Dobson, *Love Must Be Tough* (Dallas: Word, 1990).

[28]C. Peter Wagner, *Your Church Can Grow* (Ventura, Calif.: Regal, 1976), p. 35.

[29]Harvie M. Conn traces the development of McGavran's evangelistic philosophy of ministry in "Looking for a Method: Backgrounds and Suggestions," in *Exploring Church Growth*, ed. Wilbert R. Shenk (Grand Rapids, Mich.: Eerdmans, 1983), pp. 80-85.

[30]Donald McGavran, *Understanding Church Growth* (Grand Rapids, Mich.: Eerd-mans, 1990), p. 31.

[31]Ibid., p. 30.

[32]Win Arn and Charles Arn. *The Master's Plan for Making Disciples* (Monrovia, Calif.: Church Growth, 1982), p. 20.

[33]Win Arn and Charles Arn, "The State of Evangelism in America," in *The Pastor's Church Growth Handbook*, ed. Win Arn (Pasadena, Calif.: Church Growth, 1979), 2:15-20.

[34]John R. W. Stott, *What Christ Thinks of the Church* (Grand Rapids, Mich.: Eerd-mans, 1958), p. 26.

[35]Rick Warren, *The Purpose-Driven Church* (Grand Rapids, Mich.: Zondervan, 1995), p. 86.

Chapter 6: The Good Shepherd

[1]Rick Warren, *The Purpose-Driven Church* (Grand Rapids, Mich.: Zondervan, 1995), p. 86.

[2]Three outstanding resources for study that will assist you in developing your phi-losophy of ministry are Warren, *The Purpose-Driven Church;* Stephen Macchia, *Becoming a Healthy Church* (Grand Rapids, Mich.: Baker, 1999); Leith Anderson, *A Church for the 21st Century* (Minneapolis: Bethany House, 1992). Two excellent books that will help you to understand the dynamics of attracting seekers are Lee Strobel, *Inside the Mind of Unchurched Harry and Mary* (Grand Rapids, Mich.: Zondervan, 1993); and George Barna, *User Friendly Churches* (Ventura, Calif: Regal, 1991).

[3]Ronald J. Sider, *Rich Christians in an Age of Hunger: A Biblical Study* (Downers Grove, Ill.: InterVarsity Press, 1977), p. 107.

[4]Ibid.

[5]Ibid.

[6]One of the great things the Root Cellar has done is offer classes to the resident of the Munjoy Hill area, teaching them how to read, write, shop, cook healthy meals and grow in their faith in God. In this process the Root Cellar offers many oppor-tunities for laity from area churches to participate in this training. This provides excellent hands-on ministry opportunities for the people in the church.

[7]Carl George, lecture presented in Richard Wagner's Church Growth I class at Fuller Theological Seminary, March 4-14, 1991.

[8]Ronald M. Enroth, *Churches That Abuse* (Grand Rapids, Mich.: Zondervan, 1992), p. 128.

[9]Ibid., pp. 128-29.

[10]Charles Colson and Ellen Santilli Vaughn, *The Body* (Dallas: Word, 1992), p. 92.

[11]Ibid., p. 93.

[12]Ibid., p. 149.

[13]Ibid., p. 150.

[14]Ibid.

[15]Thelma Geer, *Mormonism, Mama and Me* (Chicago: Moody Press, 1986), pp. 50-51.

Epilogue

[1]<www.cp-tel.net/miller/BilLee/quotes/Troosevelt.html>.

Bibliography

Anderson, Leith. *A Church for the 21st Century*. Minneapolis: Bethany House, 1992.

Anderson, Ray S. *Ministry on the Fireline*. Downers Grove, Ill.: InterVarsity Press, 1993.

Arn, Win, ed. *The Pastor's Church Growth Handbook*. 2 vols. Pasadena, Calif.: Church Growth, 1979.

Arn, Win and Charles Arn. *The Master's Plan for Making Disciples*. Monrovia, Calif.: Church Growth, 1982.

Arnold, Matthew. "Stanzas from the Grand Chartreuse." 1855.

Baker, Don. *Beyond Forgiveness*. Portland, Ore.: Multnomah Press, 1984.

Barna, George. News Release. Barna Research Group. February 28, 1996.

Bassham, Rodger C. *Mission Theology, 1948-1975: Years of Worldwide Creative Tension—Ecumenical, Evangelical and Roman Catholic*. Pasadena, Calif.: William Carey Library, 1979.

Bellah, Robert N., et. al. *Habits of the Heart: Individualism and Commitment in American Life*. Berkeley: University of California Press, 1985.

Berger, Peter L. *A Rumor of Angels*. New York: Anchor, 1990.

Berkley, James D. "Church Growth Comes of Age." *Leadership* 12 (Fall 1991).

Bloesch, Donald G. *The Reform of the Church*. Grand Rapids, Mich.: Eerdmans, 1970.

Bonhoeffer, Dietrich. *Life Together*. San Francisco: Harper & Row, 1954.

_____. "Disillusioned with Your Church?" *Leadership* (Winter 1998).

Borthwick, Paul. *A Mind for Missions*. Colorado Springs: NavPress, 1987.

Bugbee, Bruce, Don Cousins, and Bill Hybels. *Network*. Grand Rapids, Mich.: Zondervan, 1994.

Bunyan, John. *Pilgrim's Progress*. Reprint, North Brunswick, N.J.: Bridge-Logos, 1998.

Burks, Ron, and Vicki Burks. *Damaged Disciples*. Grand Rapids, Mich.: Zondervan, 1992.

Calvin, John. *Institutes of the Christian Religion*. Edited by J. T. McNeill. 2 vols. Philadelphia: Westminster Press, 1960.

Cho, Paul Yonggi. *Successful Home Cell Groups*. South Plainfield, N.J.: Bridge, 1981.

Colson, Charles, and Ellen Santilli Vaughn. *The Body*. Dallas: Word, 1992.

Coniaris, Anthony M. *Introducing the Orthodox Church*. Minneapolis: Light and Life, 1982.

Dawn, Marva J. *Reaching Out Without Dumbing Down: A Theology of Worship for the Turn-of-the-Century Culture*. Grand Rapids, Mich.: Eerdmans, 1995.

Dobson, James. *Love Must Be Tough*. Dallas: Word, 1990.

Draper, Edythe. *The Almanac of the Christian World*. Wheaton, Ill.: Tyndale House, 1990.

Enroth, Ronald M. *Churches That Abuse*. Grand Rapids, Mich.: Zondervan, 1992.

Fee, Gordon. *The First Epistle to the Corinthians*. New International Commentary on the New Testament. Grand Rapids, Mich.: Eerdmans, 1987.

Gaebelein, Frank E., ed. *The Expositor's Bible Commentary*. Volume 3. *Deuteronomy-2 Samuel*. Grand Rapids, Mich.: Zondervan, 1992.

———. *The Expositor's Bible Commentary*. Volume 11, *Ephesians, Philippians, Colossians, 1, 2 Thessalonians, 1, 2 Timothy, Titus, Philemon*. Grand Rapids, Mich.: Zondervan, 1978.

Geer, Thelma. *Mormonism, Mama and Me*. Chicago: Moody Press, 1986.

George, Carl F. *Prepare Your Church for the Future*. Grand Rapids, Mich.: Revell, 1993.

Getz, Gene. *Building Up One Another*. Wheaton, Ill.: Scripture Press, 1976.

Goetz, David. "Tour of Duty." *Leadership* 17 (Spring 1996).

Guinness, Os. *Dining with the Devil*. Grand Rapids, Mich.: Baker, 1993.

Haggard, Ted. *Primary Purpose: Making It Hard for People from Your City to Go to Hell*. Orlando, Fla.: Creation House, 1995.

Hendricks, William D. *Exit Interviews*. Chicago: Moody Press, 1993.

Henry, Carl F. H. "Churches and Christian Fellowship." *Basic Biblical Beliefs: Six Foundational Christian Doctrines*. Teaching sessions. In Charles Colson. *The Body*. Dallas: Word, 1992.

Hoge, Dean R., and David A. Roozen, eds. *Understanding Church Growth and Decline, 1950-1978*. New York: Pilgrim, 1979.

Hordern, William E. *A Layman's Guide to Protestant Theology*. New York: Macmillan, 1955.

John Paul II. *Crossing the Threshold of Hope*. New York: Alfred A. Knopf, 1994.

Kaldor, Peter, et al. *The Winds of Change: The Experience of Church in a Changing Australia*. Sydney: Anzea, 1994.

Kennedy, D. James. *Evangelism Explosion*. Wheaton, Ill.: Tyndale House, 1983.

Kenneson, Phillip, and James Street. *Selling Out the Church*. Nashville: Abingdon, 1997.

Kittel, Gerhard, and Gerhard Friedrich, eds. *Theological Dictionary of the New Testament*. Translated by G. W. Bromiley. 10 vols. Grand Rapids, Mich.: Eerdmans, 1965-1985.

Lewis, C. S. *The Screwtape Letters*. New York: Macmillan, 1961.

Macchia, Stephen. *Becoming a Healthy Church*. Grand Rapids, Mich.: Baker, 1999.

Martin, Ralph P. "Church Growth Is Not the Point." *Life of Faith,* January 10, 1976.

Martin, Walter. *The Kingdom of the Cults*. Minneapolis: Bethany House, 1985.

McGavran, Donald. *The Bridges of God: A Study in the Strategy of Missions*. London: World Dominion, 1955.

———. *Understanding Church Growth*. Grand Rapids, Mich.: Eerdmans, 1990.

McGavran, Donald, and C. Peter Wagner. *Your Church and Church Growth: A Self-Study Course*. Revised edition. Pasadena, Calif.: Charles E. Fuller Institute of Evangelism and Church Growth, 1982.

Minear, Paul. *Images of the Church in the New Testament*. Philadelphia: Westminster Press, 1977.

Murren, Doug. *The Baby Boomerang*. Ventura, Calif.: Regal, 1990.

Neuhaus, Richard John. *Freedom for Ministry*. Grand Rapids, Mich.: Eerdmans,

1992.

Newbigin, Lesslie. *The Open Secret: Sketches for a Missionary Theology.* Grand Rapids, Mich.: Eerdmans, 1978.

Padilla, C. René. "A Steep Climb Ahead for Theology in Latin America." *Evangelical Missions Quarterly* 7, no. 2 (1971).

Patterson, Robert. "In Search of the Visible Church." *Christianity Today,* March 11, 1991.

Schaller, Lyle. *It's A Different World.* Nashville: Abingdon, 1987.

Shenk, Wibert R., ed. *Exploring Church Growth.* Grand Rapids, Mich.: Eerdmans, 1983.

Sider, Ronald J. *Rich Christians in An Age of Hunger: A Biblical Study.* Downers Grove, Ill.: InterVarsity Press, 1977.

Slosser, Bob. *Miracle in Darien.* Plainfield, N.J.: Logos International, 1979.

Snyder, Howard A. *Community of the King.* Downers Grove, Ill.: InterVarsity Press, 1977.

Stott, John R. W. *What Christ Thinks of the Church.* Grand Rapids, Mich.: Eerdmans, 1958.

Strobel, Lee. *Inside the Mind of Unchurched Harry and Mary.* Grand Rapids, Mich.: Zondervan, 1993.

Taber, Clinton E. "Report of Superintendent, Eastern Regional Association, Advent Christian General Conference." Portsmouth, N.H. October 16, 1998.

Van Engen, Charles. *God's Missionary People: Rethinking the Purpose of the Local Church.* Grand Rapids, Mich.: Baker, 1995.

Wagner, C. Peter. Church Growth I. Lecture notes. Pasadena, Calif.: Fuller Theological Seminary, March 1991.

———. *Church Growth and the Whole Gospel: A Biblical Mandate.* San Francisco: Harper & Row, 1981.

———. *Understanding Church Growth.* 3rd edition. Grand Rapids, Mich.: Eerdmans, 1990.

———, ed. *Church Growth: State of the Art.* Wheaton, Ill.: Tyndale House, 1986.

Warren, Rick. *The Purpose-Driven Church.* Grand Rapids, Mich.: Zondervan, 1995.

Waymire, Bob, and C. Peter Wagner. *The Church Growth Survey Handbook.* Milpitas, Calif.: Global Church Growth, 1984.

Weber, Hans-Reudi. "God's Arithmetic." *Frontier* 6 (Winter 1963).

Wells, David F. *God in the Wasteland.* Grand Rapids, Mich.: Eerdmans, 1994.

———. *Losing Our Virtue.* Grand Rapids, Mich.: Eerdmans, 1998.

West, Cornel. "The '80s Market Culture Run Amok." *Newsweek,* January 3, 1994.

Wuthnow, Robert. *Sharing the Journey: Support Groups and America's New Quest for Community.* New York: Free Press, 1994.

Yancey, Philip. "Taking My Stand with the Church." *Leadership* 17 (Spring 1996).

Zunkel, C. Wayne. *Church Growth Under Fire.* Scottsdale, Penn.: Herald, 1987.